BIBLE DEVOTIONS
FOR KIDS

BIBLE DEVOTIONS
FOR KIDS

180 DAYS OF WISDOM AND ENCOURAGEMENT

EMILY BIGGERS

BARBOUR
kidz

© 2020 by Barbour Publishing, Inc.

Print ISBN (*Bible Devotions for Girls*) 978-1-63609-684-1
Print ISBN (*Bible Devotions for Boys*) 978-1-63609-683-4

Scripture quotations, unless otherwise noted, are taken from the New Life Version (NLV) copyright © 1969 and 2003 by Barbour Publishing, Inc. All rights reserved.

Scripture quotations marked NIV are taken from the HOLY BIBLE, NEW INTERNATIONAL VERSION®. NIV®. Copyright © 1973, 1978, 1984, 2011 by Biblica, Inc.™ Used by permission. All rights reserved worldwide.

Scripture quotations marked KJV are taken from the King James Version of the Bible.

Published by Barbour Publishing, Inc., 1810 Barbour Drive, Uhrichsville, Ohio 44683, www.barbourbooks.com

Our mission is to inspire the world with the life-changing message of the Bible.

Member of the
Evangelical Christian
Publishers Association

Printed in China.
002145 0724 HA

SNUGGLE IN WITH THESE BIBLE DEVOTIONS AND PRAYERS. . .AND WATCH YOUR FAITH GROW!

Of all the words ever spoken, the ones we should pay the most attention to are those spoken by our Savior, Jesus Christ! These words are often set apart in red on the pages of a Bible. Throughout His ministry on earth, Jesus spoke words of healing, causing the blind to see and the lame to walk. He also spoke words of guidance, instructing believers in how to live. Some of Christ's words are promises you can claim when you face hard times. Others tell stories called parables, which help you understand important truths that Jesus wants you to know. You can even read prayers that Jesus prayed to our heavenly Father. As you jump into the daily devotions in this book, ask Jesus to lead the way. He will help you understand His words and apply them to your life today. The words of Jesus are powerful because He is the Son of God. Now, listen up! The Bible has some important things to say to you!

FISHERS OF MEN

Jesus said to them, "Follow Me. I will make you fish for men!" At once they left their nets and followed Him.

MATTHEW 4:19–20

We read about the twelve disciples of Jesus. We follow them as they follow Jesus. We hear their doubts and fears. We listen as they preach with power. We sometimes forget they were just ordinary men, many of them fishermen, before Jesus called them.

These closest friends of Jesus left a lot in order to serve with Him in ministry. They literally laid down their nets. Fishing was not just a hobby for them but was the way they earned their money. These first disciples were willing to give up everything for Jesus. He used these men to "fish for men." In other words, they drew others to Christ, and those people were saved and given eternal life. This work was much more important than fishing for fish!

Jesus still calls us to be fishers of men. Have you shared Jesus with friends at school or friends in your neighborhood who don't know Him? Have you told someone about the change Christ has caused in your own life? Start today!

Jesus, please give me the courage to speak about You to others. I want to be a fisher of men! Amen.

THIS LITTLE LIGHT OF MINE

"Let your light shine in front of men. Then they will see the good things you do and will honor your Father Who is in heaven."

MATTHEW 5:16

Have you ever sung the song, "This little light of mine, I'm gonna let it shine. . .let it shine, let it shine, let it shine"? Your light is not so *little* after all.

Think about walking through a field in the pitch black of night. You can't see anything—not even your hand in front of your face! Then, suddenly, someone turns on a flashlight. Your path is illuminated, and you can see where you are going.

Just like light from a flashlight, your good deeds shine light that points to Jesus. When you are selfless rather than selfish, people will ask why. Then you can point them to Jesus, explaining that because you love Him, you want to love others well. If the light that you shine in this world helps lead even one person to Christ, that is no small act. That is a great big victory for the kingdom of God!

Lord, help me to shine for You so that others may come
to know You and be saved from their sins. Amen.

LOVE THE UNLOVABLE

"You have heard that it has been said, 'You must love your neighbor and hate those who hate you.' But I tell you, love those who hate you. (*Respect and give thanks for those who say bad things to you. Do good to those who hate you.) Pray for those who do bad things to you and who make it hard for you."

MATTHEW 5:43–44

Loving those who love us is easy. When someone is kind to you, you want to be kind in return. But loving those who are unkind is much harder, isn't it? The words of our Savior tell us, in no uncertain terms, that we are to love our enemies. We are to repay harsh words with kind ones. We are even instructed to pray for those who do bad things to us.

This may seem impossible, but you will find that as you begin to pray for such people, your heart will soften toward them. It has been said that hurting people hurt people. In other words, those who have been hurt will often turn around and hurt others. Remember to pray for healing for those who are rude or even downright mean to you. They need Jesus to come into their hearts and change them.

Lord, help me to pray for those who are unkind to me. Right now I lift up _____ to You, and I ask that You heal the hurt in this person's heart. Amen.

YES AND NO

"I tell you, do not use strong words when you make a promise.
Do not promise by heaven. It is the place where God is.
Do not promise by earth. It is where He rests His feet.
Do not promise by Jerusalem. It is the city of the great King.
Do not promise by your head. You are not able to make
one hair white or black. Let your yes be YES. Let your no be
NO. Anything more than this comes from the devil."

MATTHEW 5:34–37

Jesus tells His followers in His holy Word to let our "yes" be "yes" and our "no" be "no." We are not to swear by using God's name or by any other person or place. You have heard people say these words: "I swear to God." Swearing to God is not necessary. We are told that such oaths are from Satan. When you make a promise, always be sure to keep it. When you do, you show that your word counts. You prove that when you say "yes," it means "yes" and not just "maybe." When you say "no" to something, do it in the same manner. Think and pray before you make decisions or statements, and when you do, let your word be enough.

Lord, I will not swear by Your name or by heaven
or earth. Give me the strength to always keep
my word and to let that be enough. Amen.

GIVE IN SECRET

*"When you give, do not let your left hand
know what your right hand gives."*

Matthew 6:3

Have you ever heard someone brag about how much he gives? Have you heard a friend tell a group about her large donation to charity or the great things she has done to help those in need? Doesn't that just seem wrong to you? There is a reason it seems wrong to boast about our giving—it *is* wrong!

Jesus tells us in the book of Matthew that we are not to stand up and make a big deal about the money we give to the church or to the poor. Our giving is to be a private thing. It is to come from the heart and not be for show or attention. Remember this the next time you feel led to give. Be generous in your giving. Your generosity pleases your heavenly Father. But try to keep the amount of your gift between the two of you. No one else needs to know. You will be rewarded in heaven one day for this type of quiet giving.

Jesus, as I give, may I do so in a private way. When I am tempted to tell others so that I will look good, remind me of Your command to give in secret. May my giving please You and may my attitude always be right. Amen.

PRAY IN SECRET

"When you pray, do not say the same thing over and over again making long prayers like the people who do not know God. They think they are heard because their prayers are long. Do not be like them. Your Father knows what you need before you ask Him."

MATTHEW 6:7–8

Just as our Lord tells us to give in secret, He also instructs us to pray in secret. There are those who like to use big words and go on and on in their prayers. Is this type of prayer truly for God's ears, or is it for other people to hear and be impressed?

God is not interested in how long your prayers are. He doesn't care if you use big words or very simple ones. He wants to have a relationship with you. He wants you to talk with Him at the start and the close of each day. He wants you to come to Him in prayer all throughout the day as well. We are told to go into a closet and pray in secret. You can pray anywhere—in the car, in a classroom, while you wait in a long line. . .anywhere. Jesus wants your heart more than He desires your fancy words. He already knows your needs. He just wants you to come and meet with Him in private prayer every day.

Jesus, may my prayers be for You and not for others to notice my fancy words. I love You. Amen.

THE LORD'S PRAYER

"Pray like this: 'Our Father in heaven, Your name is holy.
May Your holy nation come. What You want done, may it be
done on earth as it is in heaven. Give us the bread we need today.
Forgive us our sins as we forgive those who sin against us.
Do not let us be tempted, but keep us from sin. Your nation is holy.
You have power and shining-greatness forever. Let it be so.'"

MATTHEW 6:9–13

Jesus gave us a prayer that we are to pray. It is often called the Lord's Prayer. Have you heard it? As you read through the words of this prayer, stop to think about what they mean. Rather than just reciting the words, speak them from your heart.

The first part honors God as holy and acknowledges Him as our Father. The prayer says that God's will—whatever it is—should be done on earth as it is in heaven. You are asking God to give you what you need day by day and to forgive your sins as you forgive others' sins against you. You are asking Him to protect you from being tempted to sin. You are declaring that His kingdom is holy and that He has all the power and glory. These are powerful words. Commit them to memory. Pray them. Jesus told us to.

Jesus, thank You for this model prayer that teaches
me what is important in prayer. May I truly mean these
words as I speak them now in prayer before You. Amen.

ONLY ONE BOSS

"No one can have two bosses. He will hate the one and love the other. Or he will listen to the one and work against the other. You cannot have both God and riches as your boss at the same time."

MATTHEW 6:24

Have you ever tried to play a game or complete a task when everyone wants to be the leader? Arguments break out and nothing is clear or understood. Nothing gets accomplished because of the confusion and chaos.

That's why Jesus tells us in His word that we can have only one leader. There is room in your life for only one boss. Who will it be? Will you make God your ruler, or will you choose to let riches rule you?

You may think to yourself, *I'm not rich. I don't have a lot of money or treasures. How could I be ruled by riches?* But think again. *Riches* can mean anything that is of this world. Do video games or trendy clothes have an important place in your life? Is your cell phone super important to you? Do you have collections or trophies that mean a lot to you? Anything that comes before God in your life attempts to be your "boss." You can have only one master and leader in life. Choose God because He will never let you down.

Jesus, I know the things of this world are just temporary.
While I enjoy some of them, may I never let them
be more important than You in my life. Amen.

DO NOT WORRY

*"Do not worry. Do not keep saying, 'What will we eat?' or,
'What will we drink?' or, 'What will we wear?' The people
who do not know God are looking for all these things.
Your Father in heaven knows you need all these things."*

MATTHEW 6:31–32

A popular song some years back featured the lyrics "Don't worry,
be happy." The words became well-known and were often repeated
with a smile in order to encourage a friend. Jesus encourages us not
to worry. In the book of Matthew, He tells us that we should not go
around asking about what we will eat or drink or wear. God knows
our needs and is ready to meet them. Just as God puts beautiful
flowers in a field, He will provide you with clothing to wear. Just as
He makes sure the birds have food, He will certainly make sure you
don't go hungry. Trust in the Lord to meet your needs day by day.

Have you heard the old saying, "Don't borrow trouble"? This is
good advice because Christ Himself said that each day has enough
trouble of its own. He tells us not to worry needlessly because our
heavenly Father is in control of all things.

Lord, I tend to worry about the future.
Help me instead to focus on one day at a time
and to put my trust in You to meet my needs. Amen.

EXAMINE YOUR OWN HEART

"Why do you look at the small piece of wood in your brother's eye, and do not see the big piece of wood in your own eye? How can you say to your brother, 'Let me take that small piece of wood out of your eye,' when there is a big piece of wood in your own eye? You who pretend to be someone you are not, first take the big piece of wood out of your own eye. Then you can see better to take the small piece of wood out of your brother's eye."

MATTHEW 7:3–5

Have you ever listened in as young children played in a sandbox or on a playground? Often, one child will correct another child for something he is also guilty of. "Don't take all the buckets!" a little boy shouts at his friend, while hoarding all of the shovels himself.

As we get older, we are often guilty of the same behavior. Before you point out someone else's weakness, take a good, hard look in the mirror. In other words, examine your own heart rather than making a big deal of someone else who does wrong. Work on making your actions and thoughts pleasing to the Lord. We are all sinners and fall short of the glory of God. Spend your time building others up rather than looking for what they do wrong.

Jesus, give me eyes to see the good in others. Help me to point out what they do right, rather than their sins. Amen.

JESUS CALMS A STORM

He said to them, "Why are you afraid? You have so little faith!" Then He stood up. He spoke sharp words to the wind and the waves. Then the wind stopped blowing.

MATTHEW 8:26

Have you ever been afraid? The disciples of Jesus were scared during a bad storm while they were on a boat. The waves were strong. The wind probably howled. And where was Jesus? He was there with them, but He was sleeping! When His followers woke Him up, asking for His help, they were not just a little nervous—they were afraid they were going to die! Jesus calmly stood up and spoke to the wind and waves. He commanded the wind to stop blowing, and it did. Before their very eyes, Jesus' friends witnessed a miracle. Can you imagine their mouths dropping open in awe? The next verse of scripture says that Jesus' followers "were surprised and wondered about it. They said, 'What kind of a man is He? Even the winds and the waves obey Him.'" Jesus has the power to stop a storm in its tracks. He can handle any problem you lay before Him. Give Him your worries today.

Jesus, please calm the storm that is in my heart and mind in the same way that You calmed the storm on the lake when the disciples sought Your help. Amen.

JESUS OFFERS YOU REST

*"Come to Me, all of you who work and have
heavy loads. I will give you rest."*

MATTHEW 11:28

Have you ever tried to carry a load that was too heavy for you? Maybe it was a bag of groceries that spilled and cans of beans and corn rolled all over the kitchen floor. Perhaps your school backpack has been so loaded with books and school supplies that it was hard to carry. All of us have carried heavy loads before, and at times we have needed help. Isn't it nice when someone comes along and takes that heavy suitcase or bag out of your hands? "Let me carry that," she says, and suddenly your load is lightened. You breathe again and sigh with relief.

Jesus wants to relieve you of a different type of load. He offers to take on your worries, your fears, and even your sin. Cast your cares on Him, for He cares for you. Find rest in Jesus today. He offers it freely to those who will simply accept His help.

Lord, please help me to lay down the load I am carrying
day after day. As I give You my concerns, may I trust
You enough to never pick them up again. Amen.

JESUS HEALED ON THE SABBATH

He said to them, "If one of you has a sheep which falls into a hole on the Day of Rest, will you not take hold of it and pull it out? How much better is a man than a sheep! So it is right to do good on the Day of Rest."

MATTHEW 12:11–12

The proud religious law-keepers were trying to trap Jesus. They watched Him heal a man on the Sabbath—the Day of Rest—which was to be kept holy by resting on that day. Jesus compared the man to a sheep who had fallen into a pit on the Sabbath. Wouldn't they go after the sheep even though such a rescue would require them to work? He showed clearly that it was more important to do the right thing and help this person who was in need, rather than keeping the letter of the law, which commanded rest on the Sabbath. The religious teachers were just looking for something to hold against Jesus. They wanted a reason to have Him arrested and even killed. Instead of praising the Lord as the man was healed right before their eyes, they plotted against Jesus.

Thank Jesus today for His healing work in your life. Ask Him to make you sensitive to the needs of those around you.

Lord, You were always looking for those who needed a healing touch. Thank You for saving me from sin and healing my heart. Give me opportunities to serve and minister to others, I ask. Amen.

WORDS ARE IMPORTANT TO JESUS

"I say to you, on the day men stand before God, they will have to give an answer for every word they have spoken that was not important. For it is by your words that you will not be guilty and it is by your words that you will be guilty."
MATTHEW 12:36–37

Words matter. You have heard it said that "sticks and stones may break your bones, but words will never hurt you." That's not true, is it? Words have the power to sting and even to wound very deeply. Do you remember some harsh or ugly words that were spoken to you in the past? Words stay with us. They can build us up or tear us down.

Words are important to Jesus. In the book of Matthew, Jesus warns that one day each person will have to give an answer for the words he has spoken. Be sure that the words you speak today serve a purpose. Make this the test before you choose to speak: *Are the words I am about to speak true? Are they loving? Are they helpful?* If you cannot answer yes to these questions, then your words are better left unspoken.

Lord, help me to use my words to build others up and never to tear them down. I want to use my words today and every day to honor You. Amen.

WHAT CAN YOU OFFER TO JESUS?

They said to Him, "We have only five loaves of bread and two fish." Jesus said, "Bring them to Me."
MATTHEW 14:17–18

What talents and abilities do you have? What possessions do you own? What can you offer to Jesus, even if it seems small or unimportant? On a hillside one day, a boy had only a small lunch to offer. He had some bread and fish. What kind of gift was this for the King? But when the Son of God asked what food was available, the boy gave his lunch. He handed it over to Jesus. Jesus prayed and performed a miracle that day, feeding over five thousand men, women, and children. Thousands were fed from that one small lunch!

Imagine giving what you have to the Lord. He can transform even the smallest gift into so much more. He may choose to use your musical ability or your outgoing personality in ways you can't even imagine. He may use your talent in soccer or art or even your allowance to do great things for His kingdom. Consider what you have that you need to give to Jesus. He can make much of what seems like little!

Lord, I give You my ___ (list your special talents, abilities, or possessions). I offer You all that I have and all that I am. I want to be useful to Your kingdom. Amen.

TRUST JESUS

Jesus said, "Come!" Peter got out of the boat and walked on the water to Jesus. But when he saw the strong wind, he was afraid. He began to go down in the water. He cried out, "Lord, save me!"

MATTHEW 14:29–30

Jesus was walking on water. Wait—walking *on* water? That was possible only because He was the Son of God. He called to Peter, who was on the boat, to come out and join Him. Peter saw Jesus and focused on Him. He stepped out of the boat, and he too walked upon the surface of the water. But in the next moment, Peter noticed something else: the wind. His focus moved from the Savior to the wind. As fear replaced his faith, Peter began to sink.

We read this story and shake our heads in disappointment. Why didn't Peter just trust Jesus?! Yet we do the same. Jesus has called each of us into some unknown territory—a place where we must trust Him to see us through. When He calls you to share the gospel in your school or to say no to something all your friends are doing, step out in faith. When He asks you to go on a mission trip or give up your video games or social media, step out in faith.

Keep your eyes on Jesus and not on the impossible. With Christ, all things are possible. Even walking on water!

Jesus, help me to be sensitive to Your call that I might go where You lead and keep my eyes fixed on You alone to see me through. Amen.

PRAYING WITH OTHER BELIEVERS

*"For where two or three are gathered
together in My name, there I am with them."*
Matthew 18:20

Do you sometimes choose to get by yourself and pray? This is pleasing to God. The Lord tells us in His Word to go into a closet and offer up a humble prayer, not one with fancy words repeated over and over. But we are also told to seek the Lord together in prayer. In this verse, we are told that when believers come together and pray, the Lord is there with them.

What do you need to ask others to pray for? Do you have family members or a church group who will come together in prayer? Make it a point to pray together with other people who follow Christ. There is so much power in this type of prayer. Intercede for one another. Praise and thank God. Ask Him to strengthen you as individuals and as a group of Christians who are seeking Him together. Wherever two or more are gathered in the name of Jesus Christ, He is there with them. What a promise!

Jesus, thank You for the other believers You have put in my life.
May I make prayer a priority in my life—both private prayer
and prayer with groups of Christian brothers and sisters. Amen.

JESUS LOVES KIDS

*Then little children were brought to Him that He might
put His hands on them and pray for them. The followers
spoke sharp words to them. But Jesus said, "Let the
little children come to Me. Do not stop them. The holy
nation of heaven is made up of ones like these."*

MATTHEW 19:13–14

Do you ever feel like you are too young for something? Maybe it's
a sport you want to play or a goal you'd like to reach. You watch
others play or accomplish the goal, and you wish you were older or
bigger. Do you ever wonder if you might be too young for Jesus to
care about you? Too young to pray? Maybe Jesus is too busy with
more important things. Maybe He is only for grown-ups. But rest
assured that is not the case.

When people were bringing children to Jesus for Him to lay His
hands on them and pray for them, the disciples stopped them. They
probably said something like, "Jesus is busy with other things. Take
those children away from Him! He doesn't have time for that!" But
Jesus stepped in. He told His disciples not to stop them. He said to
let the little children come to Him. He laid His hands upon them and
prayed for them. The Son of God has time for you. He is interested in
your fears and worries. He wants to spend time with you. Never believe
for a moment that you are too young for Jesus to care about you.

Jesus, thank You that You have time for kids. Amen.

LOVE GOD AND LOVE PEOPLE

Jesus said to him, " 'You must love the Lord your God with all your heart and with all your soul and with all your mind.' This is the first and greatest of the Laws. The second is like it, 'You must love your neighbor as you love yourself.' "
MATTHEW 22:37–39

Love God and love people. That's what it all boils down to. Love God with all you have—all your heart, soul, and mind. That is a lot of love. That is love that takes time and effort. That is not just a Sunday-only kind of love. Giving love one day a week when you go to church is not enough. God wants a relationship with you. He wants you to meet with Him, read His Word, and pray. He wants to be number one in your life. He wants to be the driver, not just sitting in the passenger seat. God also commands you to love your neighbor as yourself. Who is your neighbor? Your neighbor is not just the person who lives in the next house or apartment. Your neighbor can be a classmate, a friend, or even a teacher. Your neighbor is anyone who crosses your path in your daily life. You can show love to others by helping them, playing with them when they seem lonely, or sharing your money and possessions with them. Love God and love others. This pleases your heavenly Father.

Lord, help me to love You more each day. And please show me ways that I can love my neighbors well. Amen.

JESUS IS COMING BACK

*"You must be ready also. The Son of Man is coming
at a time when you do not think He will come."*

MATTHEW 24:44

Surprise parties are a lot of fun! Both sides of the surprise are exciting! Jumping out and shocking the birthday boy or girl is always a blast, but so is walking into a quiet room that, a moment later, fills with smiling faces and shouts of "Happy birthday!"

The Bible tells us no one knows when Jesus will return. It will be a surprise. Only God knows when Jesus is coming back. In a way, this type of surprise can seem a bit frightening. There are some unknowns for us about the second coming of Christ. The good news is that if you have accepted Jesus as your Savior and you are living for Him every day, you have nothing to fear.

What do you want to be doing when Jesus comes back? Wouldn't it be awesome if Jesus found you serving others and sharing the good news of salvation when He returns? The Bible tells us to be ready. Make sure you are using your time wisely and living in such a way that you would be happy for Jesus to come back at any moment.

Jesus, help me not to fear but to look forward to Your second coming. Help me to be ready for that wonderful surprise! Amen.

AN EXTRAVAGANT GIFT

"For sure, I tell you, wherever this Good News is preached in all the world, this woman will be remembered for what she has done."

MATTHEW 26:13

A certain woman from Bible times is still remembered today.

In fact, Jesus Himself said she would be remembered. Her name is Mary, and she lived in the town of Bethany. When Jesus came to her house, she did something that many disapproved of. She took a bottle of expensive perfume and honored Jesus by washing His feet with it. It was very valuable perfume and could have been sold for a lot of money. People scolded Mary, saying that she could have helped the poor with that money instead. But Jesus appreciated her act of love. He said that what she had done was right.

What gift can you offer the Lord? Perhaps it is a gift of time. Others might not understand why you want to go on a mission trip or serve at your church instead of hanging out with friends and playing video games all day. Give like Mary gave to Jesus. She gave the very best she had to offer. She did not hold some back for herself. She poured out all the perfume. She emptied the bottle. She gave it all to Jesus.

Jesus, I want to live out my love for You every day. Help me be one who loves You wholeheartedly and never holds back. Amen.

PRAYING FOR GOD'S WILL

He went on a little farther and got down with His face on the ground. He prayed, "My Father, if it can be done, take away what is before Me. Even so, not what I want but what You want."

MATTHEW 26:39

Have you seen a little kid's temper tantrum? Often, the cause of a young child's anger is that he is not getting what he wants. He can't have the candy until after dinner, or he is not allowed to stick his finger in the electrical outlet. It is human nature to want *what* we want *when* we want it! But as Christians, we should pray not for our own will and desires but for God's will to be done.

Praying for God's will may not feel natural or normal to you at first. You may feel strongly that a certain goal or desire *must* be God's will for you when, in fact, He has other plans. When we become open to God's will for our lives, we will always receive His very best. Even Jesus Himself prayed for the Father's will just before He was taken away by the soldiers and led to His death. He asked if there could be another way, but God knew this was the only way to save humankind. God's will was carried out because Christ was obedient to God's greater plan.

Lord, help me to pray according to Your will above my own, and remind me that Your will is always best even when I cannot see it at the time. Amen.

THE GREAT COMMISSION

Jesus came and said to them, "All power has been given to Me in heaven and on earth. Go and make followers of all the nations. Baptize them in the name of the Father and of the Son and of the Holy Spirit. Teach them to do all the things I have told you. And I am with you always, even to the end of the world."

MATTHEW 28:18–20

These words are called the Great Commission. These are the last recorded instructions given by Christ to His disciples. They are important words, and they are intended for believers today just as they were for early Christians.

How can you "go and make followers of all the nations"? Well, you may not go to other countries right now, but you do go into your school and into your neighborhood. You can start right now by telling the good news of the gospel to those around you.

You can share Christ with others so that they might come to know Him personally as their Savior. Even while you are a student, you can be a teacher. Teach others what you have learned by reading the Bible.

Does sharing Jesus with others feel scary to you? If you're not sure you have enough courage to witness to others, read Jesus' final words in this passage. He promises to be with you always. You are not alone. Go in the power of Christ and share the good news. Carry out the Great Commission. Start today.

God, please give me the boldness I need to share the good news of Jesus with those around me. Amen.

JESUS CAME FOR THE LOST

*Jesus heard it and said to them, "People who are well
do not need a doctor. Only those who are sick need a
doctor. I have not come to call those who are right with
God. I have come to call those who are sinners."*

MARK 2:17

✦ ✦ ✦

Some people criticized Jesus for hanging out with sinners. They
expected Him—if He truly was the Son of God—to associate with the
teachers of the law. They were shocked to see Him sharing meals
with tax collectors rather than with men who were well respected.

Jesus told them He had come for these very people. He had come
to save sinners and rescue the lost.

When Jesus was a boy, He went missing for a few days. When
His parents, Mary and Joseph, found Him in the temple, He said that
He was, of course, in His Father's house. He gave a similar response
here. He compared Himself to a doctor, explaining that naturally, He
had come for the sick, not those who were well.

Consider the people you spend your time with at school and in
your neighborhood. Certainly, your closest friends should be other
Christians. These friendships will strengthen you in your faith. But
be sure you are also seeking out those who don't know Jesus so that
you can share the gospel with them.

Jesus, I ask You to give me opportunities to share with lost
people around me the good news of salvation from sin. Amen.

BE STILL

He said to the sea, "Be quiet! Be still." At once the wind
stopped blowing. There were no more waves.

MARK 4:39

Psalm 46:10 says, "Be quiet and know that I am God. I will be honored among the nations. I will be honored in the earth." Just as Jesus calmed the storm, the Lord longs to calm our hearts. He commands us to be quiet. He tells us to rest in the knowledge that He is in control of all things. He is the same yesterday, today, and tomorrow. He demands honor as our God.

Imagine that boat tossing upon the waves, the fierce wind, and the frightened disciples. Picture it as if it were a movie on the theater screen. Jesus speaks to the sea, and the storm comes to an instant stop. No more wind. No more waves. Just peace. Just calm waters.

In the moments you have set aside to read this book, rest. Know that Jesus is God. Whatever troubled sea you are sailing upon, know that Jesus is still in control. He sees you. He knows. And He longs to calm your heart in the midst of it all.

Jesus, I know that sometimes You will calm the
storm I am facing and other times You may choose
to carry me safely through it to the other side.
Help me to trust You. Calm my spirit, I pray. Amen.

TELL YOUR STORY

Jesus got into the boat. The man who had had the demons asked to go with Him. Jesus would not let him go but said to him, "Go home to your own people. Tell them what great things the Lord has done for you. Tell them how He had pity on you."

MARK 5:18–19

There was a man named Legion who was filled with not one demon but many. Jesus cast those demons into pigs. The pigs ran wildly into the water and drowned. It must have been a sight to see! The people who saw this act were surprised. But they asked Jesus to leave! Perhaps they were afraid of His power. Perhaps they were angry that their pigs had died. Legion was surprised as well, but he did not want Jesus to leave. In fact, wherever Jesus went, he wanted to go too. He asked Jesus if he could go with Him when He left the area. Instead of allowing this, Jesus chose to use Legion in another way. Legion was to tell everyone he knew what the Lord had done for him. He was to stay among his own people. He was to tell his story.

You may feel that your story is not as powerful as Legion's—a man who had demons cast out of him. That is not true! Every story of a soul saved by grace is a miraculous story worth telling. Others may come to know Christ because they hear your story. Share the gospel. Start by simply telling others what Jesus has done for you.

Jesus, thank You for my salvation. Help me to tell my story so that others may come to know You. Amen.

JESUS HEALS

*At the same time Jesus knew that power had
gone from Him. He turned and said to the people
following Him, "Who touched My coat?"*

MARK 5:30

Jesus was not like any other man who ever walked the earth. He was fully God and, at the same time, fully a man. He walked on water, healed the sick, and restored sight to the blind. He fed thousands of people with just a small lunch of fish and bread. He multiplied the food before the very eyes of the crowd that day. He was, and is, a miracle worker.

When a woman who had struggled with a blood disease for many years reached out for help, she touched the hem of Jesus' robe—you know, the part at the very bottom where there are stitches in the material. She had great faith in the Savior and believed He was the Son of God. At the moment the woman touched Christ's robe, He called out, "Who touched Me?" Jesus stopped everything He was doing in order to heal this one woman. He wanted to know her. He wanted to see her. He cared.

Jesus, the Son of God, cares about you in the same way. He knows your name. He sees you. He hears your prayers. Keep seeking hard after Jesus. He is the Great Healer, and He still does miracles today.

*Jesus, heal my heart and mind. Make me new and clean,
just as You healed the woman with the blood disease.
Thank You for wanting to know my name and help me. Amen.*

JESUS RAISES THE DEAD

He took the girl by the hand and said,
"Little girl, I say to you, get up!"

MARK 5:41

She was dead. And then she was alive. Only Jesus can do such a thing! The girl was not sleeping—she was dead. Then Jesus told her to get up, and she did.

If Jesus can raise the dead to life, don't you think He can help you with your troubles? Lay your worries and trials at the feet of Jesus Christ today. Tell Him your heartaches. Share with Him what you are sad about. He cares so much for you. You are His little sheep, and He is the Good Shepherd. He wants only good for you. He is always near.

You may not be physically dead, but maybe a part of you has been deeply hurt and needs healing. Your heart and mind may be so caught up in troubles of the present or even the past that you are not able to enjoy life. Maybe you are not able to see the bright colors of the day, enjoy the warmth of sunshine on your face, or sing like you mean it. But Jesus can change all that.

Lord, just as You raised the dead girl to life again, I ask You to renew my heart. Bring me healing that can come only from You. Make me new. Give me joy. Amen.

A RIGHTEOUS ANGER

*He said to those who sold doves, "Take these things out of here!
You must not make My Father's house a place for buying and
selling!" Then His followers remembered that it was written in
the Holy Writings, "I am jealous for the honor of Your house."*

JOHN 2:16–17

Jesus became angry. What? Jesus. . .*angry*? How could that be? He
was the Son of God. He was without sin. Surely He was never angry.
Did He show His anger?

You bet He did. He was upset that people were selling things in
His Father's house.

Our place of worship is to be set aside as holy ground and not
used for purposes that don't honor God. In the scripture passage
above, people were not bringing their sacrifices to the Lord. Instead,
they were purchasing last-minute ones right there in the temple.
This was not right, and Jesus told them so. He told them by turning
over their tables!

There is a righteous and holy anger, and our Lord demonstrated
this when He became angry about the wrong use of the temple. Our
churches today should always and only be used in ways that honor
God and bring glory to His name.

Lord, may my church always honor Your name in the
way we use our building and our resources. Amen.

JESUS IS THE WAY

"For God so loved the world that He gave His only Son. Whoever puts his trust in God's Son will not be lost but will have life that lasts forever."

JOHN 3:16

Jesus spoke these famous words about Himself. He was talking to a proud religious law-keeper named Nicodemus. Imagine the surprise of this Jewish leader when he heard that it was not a person's good deeds or sacrifices that could save his soul. Jesus is the only way to eternal life. He is the only path to heaven. He is the only true God. He is the only choice.

Many people believe that doing good things is enough. Others leave it up to luck. They hope they will get into heaven. The Son of God came and told us how to have eternal life. He told us that He is the way, the truth, and the life and that no one comes to God except through Him.

Follow hard after Christ. Don't look to the left or to the right. Whoever trusts in Jesus will not be lost.

"Amazing grace, how sweet the sound that saved a wretch like me! I once was lost but now am found, was blind but now I see."

Lord, thank You for saving me. It is by faith and through Your grace that I have been saved. Amen.

THE LIGHT

"The Light has come into the world. And the Light is the test by which men are guilty or not. People love darkness more than the Light because the things they do are sinful. Everyone who sins hates the Light. He stays away from the Light because his sin would be found out."

JOHN 3:19–20

"This little light of mine, I'm gonna let it shine. . .let it shine, let it shine, let it shine!" It's a song every child growing up in church has sung. Light is such a pleasant thing. It gives us warmth. It shines in the darkness and guides us. It gives us hope. Yet light also exposes sin.

Jesus Christ is the only perfect man who ever walked the earth. He was without sin. He was the Light, yet He had taken the form of a human body. He was fully God, yet He was, at the same time, fully man.

If it weren't for Jesus, we would live in darkness. We would wander along wishing for a clear path, longing for a flicker of hope. Yet with Jesus, our sin is exposed. His light shines in the darkness and shows all that lingers in the deep, dark places of our souls.

Thank God for Jesus. Thank God for the forgiveness of sin and for salvation. Thank God for the Light!

Jesus, You are the Light that shines in the darkness. I choose to walk in Your light. Amen.

TO BE BORN AGAIN

*Jesus said to him, "For sure, I tell you, unless a man is
born again, he cannot see the holy nation of God."*

JOHN 3:3

The birth of a baby is a miraculous event! When a human being comes into this world, it is cause for celebration. A newborn baby is a beautiful thing to watch—his little eyes trying to focus on the big world he has entered, his tiny fingers, his loud cry that says, "Wait a minute! What is this? I was so snug and warm in the womb, and now this?!"

Jesus told Nicodemus, a teacher of the Jewish law, that a person must be born again in order to enter heaven. This idea confused Nicodemus. He didn't see how a person could enter his mother's womb a second time and experience a second birth.

The rebirth Jesus spoke of is a mysterious thing. He spoke of being born not of the flesh but of the Spirit. At your first birth, your parents likely celebrated your life. At your second birth, the angels in heaven rejoiced! Your first birth allowed you to live here on this earth, but your second birth—your spiritual birth—gives you access to the kingdom of God. You will spend eternity in heaven with Jesus if you have accepted Him and experienced a new birth.

Thank You, Jesus, for giving me new life in You.
I praise You for my spiritual birth. Amen.

THE MIRACLE WORKER

He asked them what time his boy began to get well.
They said to him, "Yesterday at one o'clock the sickness left."
The father knew it was the time Jesus had said to him, "Your son
will live." He and everyone in his house put their trust in Jesus.

JOHN 4:52–53

Jesus always has perfect timing. He shows up. He gets the job done. He is never late. He never misses the mark. When He raised Lazarus from the dead, He was right on time. While Mary and Martha believed Jesus to be late, if He had come earlier, He wouldn't have had the opportunity to do such a great miraculous work. He called a dead man back to life!

The same is true in these verses in John. Many people believed when Jesus healed a boy from far away. Jesus was not even in the same town with the sick young man. He spoke healing over the boy, and at that exact same time, the boy's health was restored. As a result, an entire family was saved.

Sometimes it takes a miraculous work to really shake people up. Jesus was no stranger to miracles. Many came to know Him as a result.

Jesus, You did miraculous works when You walked
this earth, and You still do miracles today.
May many continue to trust in You. Amen.

SEEN BY GOD

Jesus said to her, "Go call your husband and come back."
The woman said, "I have no husband." Jesus said,
"You told the truth when you said, 'I have no husband.'
You have had five husbands. The one you have now
is not your husband. You told the truth."
JOHN 4:16–18

Jesus knows you inside and out. He sees your strengths and weaknesses alike. He knows your joys and sorrows. He knows where you have failed and where you have been victorious. He sees your sin, and He loves you still.

The woman at the well was a Samaritan. Jews and Samaritans didn't get along in Jesus' day, yet He stopped and talked with this Samaritan woman. He tested her by asking her to go get her husband. She passed the test when she told Jesus the truth.

There is no hiding the truth from the Messiah. He knows all and sees all, and the amazing fact is that He loves us through it all.

The woman at the well experienced life change that day as she drew water and filled her jar. She was so carried away by her new life in Christ that she threw down her water jar and ran to share her good news!

What are you trying to hide from Jesus? Confess your sin to Him today. Come clean. Tell the truth. Find forgiveness and new life in Christ.

Thank You for always loving me, Lord. . .no matter what!

DON'T HIDE THE LIGHT

*"You are the light of the world. You cannot hide a city that is on
a mountain. Men do not light a lamp and put it under a basket.
They put it on a table so it gives light to all in the house."*

MATTHEW 5:14–15

A city on a mountain can be seen for miles and miles. All you have to
do is look up in order to see the lights of the city. A city on a mountain
would be nearly impossible to hide! The same goes for a lamp. Why
would someone turn on a lamp, which is used to provide light, only
to cover it up with a basket? How foolish that would be!

In the same way, it would be silly for Christ followers to hide their
light. Wherever you go and whatever you do, let your light shine for
the Lord. May others see your life and recognize there is something
different about you. You never know who may come to know Jesus
when he or she sees your light shining brightly for the Savior. Never
be ashamed of Jesus. He was bold enough to take our sin and go to
the cross. Be bold enough to share the light you have been given,
the Light of the World, Jesus Christ.

Lord, may my light shine before others that they might see me
live for You and praise my Father who is in heaven. Amen.

LIVING WATER THAT SATISFIES

Jesus said to her, "Whoever drinks this water will be thirsty again. Whoever drinks the water that I will give him will never be thirsty. The water that I will give him will become in him a well of life that lasts forever."

JOHN 4:13–14

During your whole life, people will promise you things to satisfy your longings. You will see advertisements online and on TV that offer happiness if you buy a certain brand of shoes or clothing. It is easy to believe that a certain game system, set of headphones, or cell phone will make you happy. It won't.

Everything will come up short. Nothing will satisfy. After a few days, weeks, or months, that thing that brought you some happiness will not be new anymore. The novelty will wear off. You will be pulling out the notepad and pen to make your Christmas list for the next holiday.

Nothing satisfies—nothing but Jesus. When Christ offered the woman at the well "living water," He offered her life. True life— abundant and eternal—is found only when we place our hope and trust in the Messiah. Stop hunting for happiness in *stuff*. Accept the joy and peace found only in Jesus Christ.

Sweet Jesus, my Savior—the Living Water and Bread of Life— satisfy me this day as nothing else can. Amen.

DON'T MISS JESUS

*The woman said to Him, "I know the Jews are looking
for One Who is coming. He is called the Christ. When
He comes, He will tell us everything." Jesus said to her,
"I am the Christ, the One talking with you!"*

JOHN 4:25–26

The woman at the well did not recognize Jesus. He had to spell it
out for her. "I am the Christ," he said, "the One talking with you!"

Imagine being at a costume party. Everyone is dressed up and
no one is easily identified. You chat with Darth Vader. Or maybe
a minion or Rapunzel strikes up a conversation with you. After a
little while, you feel awkward. You should know these people, yet
you just cannot place them. "It's me!" your friends say, laughing.
Their identity is revealed. Suddenly, you recognize Batman as your
teammate from soccer and Snow White as that classmate who sits
behind you in math class.

Don't miss Jesus. Knowing who He is—and who He is not—is vitally
important. The Bible is clear that Jesus is the Son of God, who was
born of a virgin and lived a sinless life and died on the cross in the
place of sinners—once for all. Recognize Him for who He is, and when
you do, share Him with others.

*Jesus, may I never miss You. The woman at the well was chatting
with God, yet she did not even know it. May I see You and know
You. May Your voice be familiar to me, Good Shepherd. Amen.*

SIT DOWN

Jesus said, "Have the people sit down." There was much grass in that place. About five thousand men sat down.

JOHN 6:10

We can learn a lot from these words spoken by our Savior. He told His disciples to have the people sit down. It seems like such a passive answer to the trouble at hand. Over five thousand people were on that hillside, and only one boy's small lunch was available to feed them.

Jesus prayed, and then He broke the bread, divided the fish, and fed them all—with baskets and baskets of leftovers.

"Sit down?" the disciples might have asked. Can you imagine their surprise? "But Jesus, we don't have enough to feed them all," they might have said, doubting His understanding of the circumstances. Yet He understood fully. He had a plan, if only they would trust Him.

When things seem hopeless, rest in the Lord. Sit down. Listen for His still, small voice. Ask Him to work a modern-day miracle. He is still in the business today!

Jesus, may I find rest in You as I lay down my worries and trust You. I know that You are in control. Help me never to doubt You. Amen.

BREAD OF LIFE

Jesus said to them, "I am the Bread of Life. He who comes to Me will never be hungry. He who puts his trust in Me will never be thirsty."

JOHN 6:35

Imagine never being hungry or thirsty again. Imagine if there were a meal that could satisfy for all time, a beverage that could quench our thirst forever. Never again would we rummage through the pantry for a snack or the fridge for a cold soda. We wouldn't need to. We would be full, satisfied, and content.

Jesus offers us such a life if only we will reach out and grasp it. He is the Bread of Life. People cannot live on bread alone. We need the Word of God. Jesus is that Word. He is alive, and He is enough.

Trust in Jesus, and that Savior-shaped hole in your life will be forever filled. You will no longer spend time trying to force the things of this world to fit in your Jesus spot. Money and entertainment don't satisfy. Even relationships with other believers—your parents, your friends, your siblings—will leave you longing for more. No human being can satisfy as Christ can.

*Jesus, Bread of Life, satisfy my soul
that I might hunger no more. Amen.*

FOLLOW THE LEADER

*"When the shepherd walks ahead of them,
they follow him because they know his voice."*

JOHN 10:4

Have you ever played the game Follow the Leader? Whatever the leader does, everyone else must do. Wherever the leader goes, everyone else must go. Sheep play this game every day with their shepherd. They know the shepherd's voice, and they don't question the path. They simply follow their leader.

This is the way we are called to follow Jesus. We don't need to have life all mapped out. We don't need to know all the answers. You may have many questions at this point in your life. You may wonder which teacher's class you will be in. You may wish you knew if you would make a certain sports team. You may be concerned about whom you will go to the school carnival with or if anyone will sit with you at lunch. You may think ahead to your future and have questions about college, marriage, or your career.

The good news is that Jesus walks ahead of you. All you have to do is learn the sound of His voice. Read His Word. Get to know Him. Then it will be easy to trust Him. Once you know that His heart is fully for you and never against you, trusting your Good Shepherd becomes second nature. Join in today. Follow the Leader!

*Jesus, I trust You. Help me to follow
wherever You lead me. Amen.*

THE ROBBER

*"The robber comes only to steal and to kill and to destroy.
I came so they might have life, a great full life."*

JOHN 10:10

Who is the robber spoken of in this verse? It is Satan. He has a mission in this world. He is up to no good. He wants to rob you of truth. He loves to sneak in and find your weak spots. Just as he tricked Adam and Eve in the garden, Satan is alive and well today. He calls out to you that what he has to offer is better than what God says. "Eat from the tree," the serpent said, tempting the first man and woman. Soon they were chomping on forbidden fruit. Soon they had turned against God. Soon they were ashamed. They had sinned. They had fallen.

And the thief is still stealing today. He takes joy. He takes hope. He is a stealthy pickpocket, a smooth shoplifter, and an eager enemy. He stands ready to reel in his prey. Never settle for lies when you know the truth. Never give in. Never give up. Never stop believing God. God has good plans for you, but Satan, while he promises happiness, never delivers. His promises fail, while those of the Lord prevail.

Accept abundant, eternal life. Accept Jesus and reject Satan, every single time.

Jesus, protect me from the snares of the devil's schemes.
I refuse to buy into the lies he is selling. Amen.

GET TO KNOW THE GOOD SHEPHERD

"I am the Good Shepherd. I know My sheep and My
sheep know Me. I know My Father as My Father
knows Me. I give My life for the sheep."
JOHN 10:14–15

Jesus spoke these words about Himself. Jesus is your Good Shepherd. He knows you. He doesn't just know who you are. He knows your name. He knows your strengths and weaknesses. He knows your preferences, dreams, and fears. He knows where you've been and where you're going. He has great plans for your life.

Jesus wants you to know Him. The way you get to know someone is by spending a lot of time with him. That sibling, cousin, or friend who can finish your sentences for you. . .no doubt, you have spent a lot of time with that person. The same is true about your friendship with Jesus. Spend time with Him in prayer and read the Bible in order to get to know Him well.

The Good Shepherd gave His life for His sheep. Spend your life—which was purchased for you by the blood of Christ— getting to know Him. You will live a good life if you choose to know and walk closely with your Shepherd.

Good Shepherd, how I thank You for knowing me inside
out and loving me still. I cannot imagine how life would
be without Your care and protection. Help me desire
a close walk with You. I love You, Lord. Amen.

YOU ARE HELD IN YOUR FATHER'S HAND

"My Father Who gave them to Me is greater than all.
No one is able to take them out of My Father's hand."

JOHN 10:29

Have you ever run from someone, a friend or sibling, with something held tight in your hand? You grip it so hard and laugh and run, hoping you won't be caught and tackled to the ground, hoping your precious treasure won't be pried from your hand! Maybe it's some money or a piece of candy you snatched away and ran off with. But then you get caught! You feel those larger, stronger fingers pulling yours off the prized possession. It's hers now. You watch her run off with it, taunting you. The game is over. She won. You lost. You tried to hold on, but you just weren't strong enough!

Think about this. God has you in the palm of His hand. The Creator of the universe holds you tightly within His fingers. He promises in His Holy Word that He will never let you go. He tells you that nothing, absolutely nothing, is strong enough to take you from His hand. Not even death. That is some promise! Go into today and tomorrow and your easy and hard days with the knowledge that your God is a mighty protector. He will never let you go!

God, thank You that You have me in the palm of Your hand. You are such a good, good Father. Amen.

JESUS AND GOD

"My Father and I are one!"

JOHN 10:30

The Trinity is a mystery. God the Father, God the Son, and God the Holy Spirit. They are three, yet they are one. They are separate, yet they are united. They are different, yet they are the same.

Jesus told the people that He is God. He said, "My Father and I are one!" These words caused the people to become angry. They picked up stones to throw at Jesus. They had seen Him heal the sick. They had heard His great teachings filled with love and grace. Yet they did not believe. They tried to seize Jesus to take Him away, but Jesus slipped away from them. It was not His time to die.

Know that there are many things you can understand as you read God's Word. God has opened your eyes to be able to make sense of the Bible if you are a Christian. But there are some things we know only in part right now and only partly understand. One day we will know fully, just as God fully knows us. The Trinity is one of those mysteries.

For now, know this—Jesus is God. He said it, and He never lies. The Son and the Father are one.

Jesus, I believe You are one with the Father.
I trust in You even when there are some things
I cannot completely understand. Amen.

A DEAD MAN WALKING

*Then Jesus said to them, "Lazarus is dead. Because of
you I am glad I was not there so that you may
believe. Come, let us go to him."*

JOHN 11:14–15

Jesus raised His friend Lazarus from the dead. He performed this miracle for a great reason. When people saw Jesus bring a dead man back to life, many believed. When others heard this story from trusted friends who had seen it, they also believed.

The teachers of the law began to fear Jesus even more after this miracle. They worried that if people began to follow Jesus, they would lose their power. In John 11:53 we read: "From that day on they talked together about how they might kill Jesus."

This was God's plan, and it was unfolding day by day. It would eventually lead to Christ's death on the cross, the single most powerful act ever—which saves us from eternal separation from God.

Think of those new believers who accepted Christ because they saw a dead man walking again. They had buried Lazarus. They had seen him dead, and now he was alive. Think of the jaws that dropped that day and of the worship Christ received.

Jesus could have gone earlier to His friend Lazarus. He could have healed him from sickness, but He had a great purpose in raising him from death. Trust in your Savior. He always knows what He is doing.

Jesus, what a miracle You did that day! What
miracles You still perform. May I always trust
in Your timing and Your plans. Amen.

JESUS' PERSPECTIVE

Jesus said, "Let her alone. She has kept it for the time
when I will be buried. You will always have poor
people with you. You will not always have Me."

JOHN 12:7–8

Jesus doesn't always see things the way others do. His point of view is a heavenly one, not limited by earthly law or reason. When the little children came to sit on His lap and stand near Him and touch Him the way little children do, His disciples scolded them. They tried to send the kids away. Jesus was busy. They thought He didn't have time for kids! But Jesus stopped His disciples. He said to let the little children come to Him. His attitude toward the children was unexpected. It was a heavenly perspective.

Something similar occurred when a woman named Mary poured out expensive perfume at the feet of Jesus. People thought she should have sold the perfume and given the money to the poor. Jesus told them to leave her alone and said that what she had done was a beautiful and honorable thing. He appreciated her gift.

Jesus walked the earth as a man, but He was not just a man. He was God, and He is God today. Read His words. Follow Him closely. Consider His teachings. Memorize His words. Then you, like Jesus, will be able to see things from a new perspective. You will see them through the lens of Jesus.

Jesus, help me know You better so that I might see things as
You do rather than just following the ways of this world. Amen.

LIGHT OF THE WORLD

*"I came to the world to be a Light. Anyone who
puts his trust in Me will not be in darkness."*

JOHN 12:46

Jesus is the Light. He shines in the darkness. Just like a flashlight or candle illuminates a dark room, Jesus brings peace and truth and life to dark places. Without Him, there is only darkness.

Do you ever wonder why people make such bad choices? From movie stars in the news to criminals who have murdered innocent victims, we shake our heads in disbelief. Why are these bad things happening? Why do people commit such evil acts? The answer is that they are walking in darkness. When you walk in the dark, you stumble over everything. You reach out and grab onto all the wrong things. You cannot see where you are going. There is no path. There is no goal. There is only darkness.

When you allow the Light of the world, Jesus Christ, into your life, He lights it up. You don't know all the answers, but you follow a Savior who does. You hold on to the Light, and He guides you through a dark world.

Jesus, I am so thankful that I have You, the Light of the world, walking with me. I am so thankful that I no longer have to stumble through the darkness. Amen.

LOVE ONE ANOTHER

*"I give you a new Law. You are to love each other.
You must love each other as I have loved you. If you
love each other, all men will know you are My followers."*

JOHN 13:34–35

An old song called "They'll Know We Are Christians by Our Love"
is a great reminder for Christians to love others.

Jesus told His disciples on the night before He was crucified that
they were to love one another. This was a new law. It was a command
He wanted His followers to obey.

This law was important then—and now!—because when we love
one another, people see it. It stands out to them. They wonder what
this love is all about. This kind of love is attention-getting because
it puts others first in our very selfish world.

Are you working with your brothers and sisters in Christ? Are
you spreading the Good News? It's easy to find reasons to disagree
with other Christians. But instead of focusing on those kinds of things,
we should follow Jesus' rule and focus on love.

Lord, may I honor You by following Your command to love
other believers and work together as one. May people see
our good works and glorify our Father in heaven. Amen.

FAITHFULNESS

*Jesus answered Peter, "Will you die for Me? For sure,
I tell you, before a rooster crows, you will have
said three times that you do not know Me."*

JOHN 13:38

It is difficult to read the story about Peter's denial of Jesus. It is hard because we relate! We start to wag our finger at Peter, shaming him, and then we realize we must point that finger back at ourselves. How many times have we promised to be faithful to the Lord only to go astray again? How many times have we had an opportunity to witness to someone, yet we turned away, afraid to boldly proclaim that we know Jesus?

Peter had promised that he loved Jesus so much that he would die for Him, yet within twenty-four hours, he denied knowing Christ three times.

It wasn't popular to stand with Jesus on the day He was crucified. It was frightening to say, "Yes, I am one of His followers. I am one of His closest friends." What would you have done if you were Peter? You can never know. But you can begin today to practice faithfulness. Today, in your lifetime, it is becoming less and less popular to stand with Christ. Will you be bold? Ask God for the strength and courage to remain faithful to Christ. Practice faithfulness today so that you can stand firm in the future.

God, give me a bold faithfulness, I pray.
May I stand with You always. Amen.

LIFE COMES FROM THE LORD HIMSELF

"I am the Vine and you are the branches. Get your life from Me. Then I will live in you and you will give much fruit. You can do nothing without Me."

JOHN 15:5

By yourself, you cannot do anything for God. Like a branch broken off from the tree, you are powerless on your own. You must draw your life and breath from Him. He is the Vine, while you are a branch. He is your Creator and Redeemer, the one who sustains your life. When you are spending time with Him, reading His word, and praying, then you will be filled with life that flows out from the Father.

Only when you draw upon His strength can you bear fruit for the Lord. Do you want to do great things for the kingdom of God? That doesn't begin on the mission field. It starts in your prayer closet. Take your first step by opening the Word of God and reading its pages. Fill your mind and heart with the Lord Himself, and He will burst forth in all that you set your hands to do. But if you go out on your own and try to do great things for God in your own strength, you won't accomplish much.

God, You are the life that sustains me.
Flow through me and give me power to
bear much fruit for Your kingdom. Amen.

WHEN THE WORLD HATES YOU

*"If you belonged to the world, the world would love you
as its own. You do not belong to the world. I have chosen
you out of the world and the world hates you."*

JOHN 15:19

If you haven't yet, at some point you will experience some degree of persecution for being a Christ follower. It may come in the form of laughter when you refuse to go along with something that others want you to do—something that you know would dishonor God. You may be excluded from events or even have to sit alone in the school cafeteria. You may not be invited or envied or popular. That's okay.

It's better to follow hard after Jesus Christ than to follow hard after this world. This world will offer you a lot of fake happiness. It will all come up short. The only lasting joy is found in walking with the Son of God day by day, hour by hour, moment by moment.

You cannot belong to the world and to Jesus. Jesus has taken hold of your life and made you new. Through Him, you have been promised eternal life in heaven.

Jesus never promised that life would be easy. He Himself was rejected and eventually killed on a cross.

Determine today to follow Jesus, regardless of the cost.

*Jesus, when I am hated by the world, I rest in the deep,
unconditional love You have for me. Amen.*

GOD IS THE SOURCE OF LIFE

*"If you get your life from Me and My Words live in you,
ask whatever you want. It will be done for you."*

JOHN 15:7

Have you ever had a power outage at your house? When the electricity goes out, even for a short time, it can really affect life! You go to turn on the TV. Nope. No electricity means no TV. You decide you'll go to your room to draw a picture, but it's too dark without the lights! Lights require electricity too!

God is our source of life. Much like electricity, He gives us power to do good works for His kingdom. Without that source, we can't accomplish anything. Be sure that every day you plug into Him, the source! When you spend time with God and draw your life from Him, there is no limit to what you can do for the Lord.

Ask God to fill you with life and use you in mighty ways. He will open doors you never would have imagined you would have the opportunity to go through. God is the great power source!

Lord, thank You for giving me strength and power.
Thank You for being the one and only life source. Fill me
with life that I might serve You better all my life. Amen.

BEARING MUCH FRUIT

*"When you give much fruit, My Father is honored.
This shows you are My followers."*

JOHN 15:8

One way that others know you are a Christ follower is by the fruit you produce. Imagine an orchard full of trees. You look out at them and see some have a couple of apples. Others have more. Some are so loaded with apples that the branches are weighed down.

When God looks at the lives of His children, He is pleased to see us producing much fruit for the kingdom. Are you sharing the good news with others at school, in your neighborhood, or on your sports team? Are you being kind? Do you pray for missionaries? Have you thought about going on a mission trip or serving in your community? These are just some of the ways you can produce fruit for the Lord.

When you bear fruit, you honor your heavenly Father. Jesus said bearing fruit shows that we are His followers.

Which apple tree do you want to be? The one that has one or two apples or the one loaded with ripe fruit? Bear much fruit for the kingdom. Start today!

Jesus, help me to bear fruit for You everywhere
I go. May I bring honor to Your name. Amen.

THE HOLY SPIRIT

"If you love Me, you will do what I say. Then I will ask My Father and He will give you another Helper. He will be with you forever. He is the Spirit of Truth. The world cannot receive Him. It does not see Him or know Him. You know Him because He lives with you and will be in you."

JOHN 14:15–17

When Jesus went back to heaven, God sent another Helper into the world. The Holy Spirit is our Comforter and our Counselor.

There is a still, small voice that sometimes guides you. You may feel led to give, to help, and to serve. You might notice a certain scripture verse. You feel loved even though you are all alone. You make that hard call and ask a friend to forgive you. You take a chance and share the gospel with a teammate. You are never on your own. You have Him—the Holy Spirit of God—within you.

The Holy Spirit will never lead you astray or leave you alone. You will walk with this Spirit as your guide for the rest of your days. So lean in a little bit. Dare to be quiet. Listen. Trust. Follow. That is the Holy Spirit at work in your life. Oh, how blessed you are to have such a Helper.

I'm listening, God. Tell me what You want
me to do, and I'll do it. Amen.

A DIFFERENT KIND OF PEACE

"Peace I leave with you. My peace I give to you.
I do not give peace to you as the world gives.
Do not let your hearts be troubled or afraid."

JOHN 14:27

There is a kind of peace that doesn't really make sense. When you are in deep waters, you are not pulled under. When you stumble, you don't fall. When your head hits the pillow at night, you can rest. You have the peace of Christ within your very soul.

This kind of peace is not available for purchase. It cannot be found in the world, for it is not of this world. It is of another world, an unknown world. It is from heaven.

Don't be afraid. Don't worry. The peace that Jesus offers is for a lifetime. It abides with you now while you are young, and it will still be yours when you are old. You can make endless withdrawals from your peace account. It will never run dry. The sweet stillness infused into your spirit by Christ, your Savior, is not dependent on age or status or even circumstances. Like Paul, you will say that you have learned to be content in any situation. May the peace of Jesus Christ reign in your heart all your days.

Jesus, thank You for this very different kind of peace. Amen.

JESUS HAS OVERCOME THE WORLD

*"I have told you these things so you may have peace
in Me. In the world you will have much trouble.
But take hope! I have power over the world!"*

JOHN 16:33

This world is full of trouble. Even though you are young, you experience some of it, don't you? You have cried over hard things. You may have lost a friend or relative. You may have buried a beloved pet. You may have been hurt, rejected, abused, or mistreated. You have known trouble.

Jesus told His disciples, and He tells us today, that this world is full of trouble. The good news is that He has overcome the world. Jesus has power over this world that only Jesus can have.

So when you are discouraged, look up. When you feel that things are really bad, maybe they are. But you have the Son of God on your side. He offers you a peace that doesn't make sense. He guides and protects you. He knows you and loves you deeply. Trust in Jesus. Sometimes He may calm the storm that rages all around you. Other times He may choose to take your hand and lead you through the storm. Don't worry! Despite the trouble at hand, Jesus is always near, and He has conquered this world.

Thank You, Lord, that I can trust in You
even when there is trouble all around. Amen.

UNITED AS ONE

*"I am no longer in the world. I am coming to You. But these
are still in the world. Holy Father, keep those You have
given to Me in the power of Your name. Then
they will be one, even as We are One."*

JOHN 17:11

Jesus prayed for Christians to be one. He asked God to protect those
who were still in the world. When He refers to those God has given
Him, that includes you if you have come to know Christ as your Savior.

Believers will spend eternity in heaven with the Lord, but for now
we are here and we have a job to do. We are to be unified. Jesus longs
for His followers to act as one body, serving one another, valuing one
another, and encouraging one another.

Just as God and Jesus are one, believers show that they are unified
when they avoid arguments within the body of Christ. If a visitor
comes to your church and hears bickering and arguing among the
church members, will they want to come back? Will that person,
when they witness disharmony, really believe that Christians are
filled with love and grace?

Focus on ways you can get along with other Christians. Do you
need to go to someone and make things right between you? If so,
take that step today.

*Lord, help us to honor You as we seek to live
as one body, united and unified. Amen.*

JESUS PRAYS FOR HIS FOLLOWERS

"I do not ask You to take them out of the world. I ask You to keep them from the devil. My followers do not belong to the world just as I do not belong to the world. Make them holy for Yourself by the truth. Your Word is truth."

JOHN 17:15–17

Have you ever faced a tough situation? You wanted to stay home from school, but your mom or dad caught on to your act. You weren't really sick. You just wanted to avoid the vocabulary test you forgot to study for or the awkward Valentine's Day party. You were forced to face the situation rather than being allowed to escape. Your parent knew it would help to develop your character. Good would come from it, even though at the time you just wanted out!

Jesus did not ask God to take believers out of the world. Rather, He prayed for His Father to protect us from the evil one. The devil is out to deceive Christians in the same way that he tricked Adam and Eve in the garden. He is sneaky, and Jesus knows that we need supernatural strength in order to resist him.

While our souls long for heaven, we are meant to be right here for now. God knew exactly the time and place that you would be born and live. He is protecting you even now from Satan, and if you allow Him to, He will use you in mighty ways to further His kingdom.

God, thank You for protecting me from Satan's snares. Amen.

JESUS SUBMITTED TO GOD'S WILL

Then Jesus said to Peter, "Put your sword back where it belongs. Am I not to go through what My Father has given Me to go through?"

JOHN 18:11

Jesus knew it was God's plan for Him to die on the cross for our sins. Peter injured one of the soldiers who had come to take Jesus to His death. Jesus stopped Peter. He told him to put away his sword. Jesus was ready to do His Father's will, and He went without a fight. He allowed others to take Him away.

In John 10:11 Jesus said, "I am the Good Shepherd. The Good Shepherd gives His life for the sheep."

Jesus was ready at this point to lay down His life for us. He was hung on a cross between two thieves. He died a criminal's death, yet He had not committed a crime. He carried all our sin upon Himself—the sin of the world, past, present, and future. It was a heavy weight, but it was one He carried to the cross willingly. He did not fight. He did not perform a miracle to slip away from the grasp of the soldiers. He let them take Him. He gave up His life, dying that we might live. Remember the sacrifice of Jesus today.

Jesus, thank You for going to the cross for me, for dying a gruesome and painful death—that I might have abundant and eternal life with You. Amen.

JESUS THE KING

Pilate said to Him, "So You are a King?" Jesus said, "You are right when you say that I am a King. I was born for this reason. I came into the world for this reason. I came to speak about the truth. Everyone who is of the truth hears My voice."

JOHN 18:37

Jesus did not come into the world the way one might imagine a king would come. Think of the kings in storybooks. They wear golden crowns decorated with jewels. They sit proudly upon their thrones and order their servants around. They eat the finest foods and lay their heads upon the softest pillows. They have the best of everything. After all, the title "king" means something.

Jesus came into the world as a king, but He did not come as the Jews expected. Most did not recognize Him. He came as a tiny baby, born in a stable, laid in a manger for His bed. He came as a carpenter's son. His hands were rough from working alongside Joseph, His earthly father.

When Pilate questioned Jesus, our Savior answered him truthfully. And He spoke words that still ring true today. He said that everyone who is of the truth hears His voice. Today, believers can hear the voice of Jesus. We read His words in the holy scriptures, and we are led by His Holy Spirit.

Lord, thank You for coming into this world and showing us the way, the truth, and the life. Amen.

DO YOU DOUBT AS THOMAS DID?

He said to Thomas, "Put your finger into My hands.
Put your hand into My side. Do not doubt, believe!"
JOHN 20:27

Thomas is often referred to as Doubting Thomas. What a nickname! Wouldn't you hate to be called Doubting Kevin or Doubting Kayleigh? Think of the worst nickname you can imagine. This is worse. After walking with Jesus, seeing His miracles, and hearing His teachings, Thomas did not believe his eyes when he saw Jesus. Surely the man who had called forth Lazarus from death could Himself be raised from the dead! Yet Thomas wasn't so sure. He wanted proof. He needed to touch Jesus. He needed to see the wounds from the crucifixion nails.

Before you judge Thomas too harshly, consider this: How often do you doubt Jesus yourself? Do you find it hard to believe that Jesus could save that family member who has no interest in Christianity? Do you question Jesus' love for you when everything seems to go wrong? Have you ever doubted your faith, wondering if all those Bible stories are really true?

It is human nature to doubt. And while Jesus longs for us to believe, He sympathizes with our humanity. He allowed Thomas to touch His scars. He will do what it takes to prove Himself true and faithful in your life as well. Trust Him!

> Jesus, may I never doubt You. May I always trust
> in You—even when I cannot see the path and even
> when I cannot understand Your ways. Amen.

MOURNING OVER YOUR SIN

"Blessed are those who mourn, for they will be comforted."
MATTHEW 5:4 NIV

Have you lost someone very special to death? Whether it was a grand-parent, another family member, or even a beloved pet who meant a lot to you, saying goodbye is always hard. When we experience loss, a deep sadness comes over us. That is called grief, or mourning.

You have likely mourned a loss in your life. Even if no one close to you has passed away, you may have had to leave a special house, school, church, or friend when you moved away to live some-where else.

These words from the famous Sermon on the Mount are words that Jesus spoke, and they are still true today. They do not refer to mourning over a person or place. Here Jesus was talking about mourning over your sin.

Recognizing that you are a sinner should cause you to grieve. It should bring a sadness to you. Do you ever say something hateful and later wish you hadn't? Do you feel bad? That is mourning over your sin.

The good news is that Jesus calls you blessed when you see your sin and are sorry for it. He offers forgiveness to those who ask for it. You will find comfort in the salvation of the Lord.

Thank You, Jesus, that You choose to forget
my sin when I ask You to forgive it. Amen.

BLESSED ARE THE POOR IN SPIRIT

"Blessed are the poor in spirit,
for theirs is the kingdom of heaven."

MATTHEW 5:3 NIV

Poor in spirit. Those are words that may not make much sense to you. Replace the word *poor* with *humble* and you may come close to understanding what Jesus meant when He made this statement. Be humble in spirit. Have a humble attitude. In other words, don't be cocky, thinking you know it all and never do anything wrong.

The Bible clearly tells us that all have sinned and fallen short of the glory of God (Romans 3:23).

Coming to God humbly—knowing you cannot forgive yourself but must depend on Him for that—pleases the Father.

The type of sorrow the Lord is approving of here is the sadness that comes when you see your sin. You realize that you are a sinner and cannot save yourself, and you decide to do something about that by repenting. This humility honors the Lord. When you ask Him for forgiveness, you are coming before Him with a poor spirit, humbly, trusting only in Him.

God, may I be humble enough to see that I make wrong choices. I sin. May I be wise enough to repent and turn from my wrong ways and follow Jesus. Amen.

BLESSED ARE THE MEEK

"Blessed are the meek, for they will inherit the earth."
MATTHEW 5:5 NIV

Meek? Think *patient*. Think of the person who is mistreated but does not react by getting angry. Think of the person who instead knows that God will take care of things. Think of Jesus on the cross.

While Jesus grew angry when people were using His Father's house, the temple, for wrong purposes, He also was a meek man. He died on the cross, allowing our sin to be cast upon Him. He did not grow angry. He knew it was the will of the Father that He die in order to make a way for us to come to Him.

Meekness is not weakness. It doesn't mean letting others trample over you. It simply means not trampling over others. Meekness means you don't insist on receiving your rights in every case.

Look out for others. And when they get it wrong and when you are mistreated, don't grow angry. Don't push others down in order to raise yourself up as better than anyone. Don't be jealous or prideful. Live in meekness. It pleases your God.

When this verse of scripture says that the meek will inherit the earth, many believe it means the meek will receive great blessings. Some of those rewards may be in this life, and some will be in heaven.

God, help me to be meek so that I might please You
and receive blessings I cannot even imagine. Amen.

HUNGER AND THIRST

*"Blessed are those who hunger and thirst
for righteousness, for they will be filled."*

MATTHEW 5:6 NIV

You know what it means to be hungry and thirsty, right? After that long day at school or that soccer game, you really want a snack and a refreshing drink!

In Matthew, Jesus speaks of being hungry and thirsty for God's Word and for the company of other Christians. He wants us to desire—to be "hungry for"—personal righteousness. This means He wants us to desire godliness more than we desire sin.

We know we are saved by the grace of God through Jesus' death on the cross and our faith in Him. We have the righteousness of Christ if we are saved. So why do we need to hunger and thirst for this godliness? Well, we want to grow each day to be a bit more like Christ and live a life that draws others to Him.

Sometimes you will be "on fire" for the Lord. You truly will be hungering and thirsting after His ways. But then you will slip up and desire things of the world again—things that are much less important, such as winning the game or being the best at something. We slip up because we are human. We will always struggle with hungering and thirsting for the things of God versus the things of the world.

God, help me each new day to go after the things
of the Lord rather than the things of this world.
I know I will be truly satisfied only in You. Amen.

BLESSED ARE THE MERCIFUL

*"Blessed are the merciful,
for they will be shown mercy."*
MATTHEW 5:7 NIV

Have you ever played the game called Mercy? You hold up both arms and lock fingers with another person. Then you begin to twist and squeeze and try to hurt their fingers and arms so badly that they shout, "Mercy!" Whoever asks for mercy first loses the game!

Mercy is forgiveness. It is showing compassion to those in need. Like the mercy we show in a silly game when we release our friend or sibling from pain, God shows mercy to us daily. He forgives our sin when He doesn't have to do so. And He sent His Son in the greatest act of mercy and grace ever shown!

When we are compassionate, we help those in need. We include others in our game on the playground. We notice someone sitting alone and invite them to join our group. We offer a shoulder to cry on or a hand to hold. That other person doesn't *earn* your mercy. Mercy is *always* a gift.

If you live as a merciful person, you will be shown mercy. Jesus said it.

In other words, if you know the mercy of God, show mercy to others. Great joy and contentment are found in living in this godly way.

Help me, Lord, to have opportunities even this
day to show mercy. May I reflect the great
mercy You showed me on the cross. Amen.

74

PURE IN HEART

"Blessed are the pure in heart,
for they will see God."

MATTHEW 5:8 NIV

Jesus purifies our hearts. They were once dirty and blackened from sin. Jesus died on the cross, once for all. He died for the sins of humankind—past, present, and future. Jesus said the pure in heart will see God. Think about that. Because you have trusted in Christ, your heart is pure and you are able to come into the presence of a holy God. You will be granted eternal life in heaven with Him.

So. . .why are we told to be pure in heart if we have already been purified by Christ? Well, throughout our lives we mix in other desires, don't we? We begin to long after success or relationships or things. When we do that, we create for ourselves a mixed heart. It is not seeking God alone. It is, at least at times, putting other things or people above God. This is part of living in the world. This is part of being human.

Seek to put God first. Seek to live life with a heart focused only on Him. That's what it means to have a pure heart. Ask God to help you enjoy the things and the people around you without making them your focus or your idol. Seek first the Lord, above all else.

Lord, help me to live life with a heart focused
only on You and Your ways. Amen.

75

PEACEMAKERS

"Blessed are the peacemakers,
for they will be called children of God."

MATTHEW 5:9 NIV

✦ ✦ ✦

God is holy, and our sin blocks us from being with Him. If it weren't for Jesus, we would be eternally separated from a holy and perfect God. But Jesus died on the cross, taking our sin upon Himself.

As Christians, we are called to be peacemakers. We do this when we take the gospel to others. When we give ourselves to share the good news, we are blessed.

There is no real, true peace apart from knowing Christ. And only those who know Christ can share Christ with others.

Choose to be a peacemaker. Start today. The Bible says the feet of those who bring the good news of Jesus are beautiful:

How beautiful on the mountains are the feet of him who brings good news, who tells of peace and brings good news of happiness, who tells of saving power, and says to Zion, "Your God rules!" (Isaiah 52:7)

Lord Jesus, give me the desire to share You with others rather than keeping You to myself. You are the only way people can find peace with God. Send me into my world—my neighborhood, my school, my teams and clubs, even into my own family— with the gospel. Make me bold, I ask. Amen.

PERSECUTION

"Blessed are those who are persecuted because of righteousness, for theirs is the kingdom of heaven."

MATTHEW 5:10 NIV

Have you ever been teased for doing the right thing? Maybe you didn't attend a party or play in a soccer game because it interfered with Bible study time or a church service. It hurts when people laugh at us or call us names. It stings when they say things like, "Oh, I forgot you have to be at church every time they open the doors!"

Jesus assured the people He taught that rewards were in store for those who were persecuted for righteousness. You can rest assured that Jesus sees those people who hurt your feelings. He hears those insults, and He is pleased when you stand firm in your faith.

It never feels good to be mistreated. It makes us feel left out or as if we don't belong. Just remember that as a child of God, you are a citizen of heaven. You belong with God and with His people. A day will come when you will be rewarded for all of the right choices you are making now, even though some of them are difficult.

Lord, give me what it takes to stand strong in my beliefs even when others make fun of me or put me down. Amen.

THOSE WHO WERE BEFORE YOU

"Blessed are you when people insult you, persecute you and falsely say all kinds of evil against you because of me. Rejoice and be glad, because great is your reward in heaven, for in the same way they persecuted the prophets who were before you."

MATTHEW 5:11–12 NIV

Do you enjoy studying history? You know, there's a reason biography is a popular genre with kids your age as well as with adults. People like to read about people—those who have led real lives, struggled, and made a difference. We relate to other people's life stories because we are human. We all experience many of the same emotions. We all have setbacks and hope to overcome them. Reading about those who have gone before us inspires us.

We can read stories like this in the Bible. Remember how others laughed when Noah and his sons built that huge ark and there was not even a cloud in the sky?

You are going to make it! You may face persecution in your life from family members or friends who do not share your Christian faith. They may insult you, poke fun at you, or even reject you. You are not the first. For generations, Christians have experienced the same thing, and some even much worse. Some Christians have lost their lives for the sake of the cross!

Heavenly Father, knowing others who came
before me faced the same things I face today
helps me to keep on keeping on! Amen.

STAY SALTY

*"You are the salt of the earth. But if the salt loses its saltiness,
how can it be made salty again? It is no longer good for
anything, except to be thrown out and trampled underfoot."*
MATTHEW 5:13 NIV

What good is salt that isn't salty? In the ancient Middle East, during
Jesus' day, salt was very important. Jesus compared salt to His disciples
in several ways. This analogy can still be used today.

Believers in Christ can make a great difference in the world. We
have the chance to share our testimonies and to live in such a way
that blesses others and helps them see that sin is not the way to
go. Just as salt, in small amounts, was tossed out onto the land as
fertilizer, believers are thrown out into the world to produce fruit
for God. We are, in some ways, a lot like salt!

Choose, as a modern-day disciple of Christ, to have a positive
impact on the world around you. Add something positive to others'
lives in the same way that salt jazzes up a plain baked potato. Produce fruit for God. Stay salty!

Lord, help me to be a positive influence on those
around me who don't yet know You. Amen.

BEING RECONCILED

"If you take your gift to the altar and remember your brother has something against you, leave your gift on the altar. Go and make right what is wrong between you and him. Then come back and give your gift."

MATTHEW 5:23–24

Do you remember preschool? The teacher would take you by the hand and ask you to tell another student you were sorry. Perhaps you had snatched a toy from another kid. Maybe you were apologizing for saying mean words or pushing someone in line. Whatever it was, your teacher found it important for you to be reconciled to your classmate. You needed to make things right again.

Even though you are much older now and you have moved on from this type of misbehavior, this scripture verse is still an important lesson for older kids, teens, and even adults. Make things right with your Christian brother or sister before you go to God with a gift of money, talents, or time.

God wants His children to live as one. But living as one is hampered by arguments and quarrels. Be sure you do all that is possible to live at peace with those around you. Say you are sorry when you recognize that you have done wrong.

Lord, help me to make things right with others.
Give me the strength to be the one to go to
them first. Give me a spirit of peace. Amen.

YES OR NO

*"Let your yes be YES. Let your no be NO.
Anything more than this comes from the devil."*

MATTHEW 5:37

Do you hear people swearing on the Bible or swearing to God? The Lord's name and His Word are very special. In fact, they are sacred and holy. Swearing on them is not good.

A simple yes or no is all you need to give. Your word should be enough. If you are living your life in a way that shows others you are trustworthy, others will know that you will do what you say.

In the book of Matthew, we read that, in fact, going beyond saying "yes" and "no" is from the devil. Those are strong words.

Make sure that you are a promise keeper. If you say you will go to a party and then you are invited to another, stick to your original commitment. If you tell your teacher you will do an assignment, do it. If you have a track record of doing what you say will do, there will never be cause for you to use God's name in vain. Do not swear by God's name.

God, remind me to be a person of honor and integrity.
Let my "yes" and my "no" be enough. Amen.

GIVE TO THOSE WHO ASK

"Give to any person who asks you for something. Do not say
no to the man who wants to use something of yours."

MATTHEW 5:42

✦ ✦ ✦

Generosity should be evident in the life of a Christ follower. Jesus Himself instructed us not to say no to someone who wants to borrow from us.

In Matthew 5, He gives some examples. We should give more than we are asked for. We read in Matthew 5:40: "If any person takes you to court to get your shirt, give him your coat also." And we are to go the extra mile, quite literally: "Whoever makes you walk a short way, go with him twice as far" (Matthew 5:41).

You might wonder about whether the person is really needy. But maybe it's better to take the chance. The other option is not to give and then sometimes miss a true need someone has.

While we certainly cannot meet every need, we can give as we are led to those who ask us. Be generous in your giving. Looking for opportunities to give pleases the Lord.

God, give me opportunities to be generous, and help me to take them. Help me to be quick to share and give. You have given me so much. May I help others as I have the chance. Amen.

AVOID BEING LUKEWARM

"Write this to the angel of the church in the city of Laodicea: 'The One Who says, Let it be so, the One Who is faithful, the One Who tells what is true, the One Who made everything in God's world, says this: I know what you are doing. You are not cold or hot. I wish you were one or the other. But because you are warm, and not hot or cold, I will spit you out of My mouth.'"

REVELATION 3:14–16

In the book of Revelation, Jesus warns against being lukewarm. Hot water cleanses. Cold water refreshes. But what good is lukewarm water? It is of no benefit. In the same way, a lukewarm Christian is worthless to the Lord.

The warning is strong. If believers are not hot or cold, Jesus says He would rather just spit them out of His mouth. That doesn't sound very pleasant, does it? That's because being lukewarm does not please Jesus.

So what does this mean for you? What is a lukewarm Christian? Those who are lukewarm are just going through the motions. They have not experienced true heart change. They are sickening to the Lord. They bring no good but instead do harm to the kingdom of God. If someone knows you claim to be a Christ follower but your actions and words don't line up with what a Christian should say and do, they won't want anything to do with Jesus.

God, I ask You to truly change my heart so that I might make a positive contribution to Your kingdom. Amen.

THE DISCIPLINE OF JESUS IS FOR YOUR GOOD

"I speak strong words to those I love and I punish
them. Have a strong desire to please the Lord.
Be sorry for your sins and turn from them."

REVELATION 3:19

No one enjoys discipline. Do your parents ever take away a privilege to teach you a lesson? Maybe you have lost electronics or been grounded. It stinks at the time, but you do learn not to repeat the same mistake!

In the book of Revelation, Jesus speaks strong words to a group of believers who need to change their ways. He loves these people. He wants them to turn away from sin and turn back to Him.

In the same way, Jesus wants us to tell Him we are sorry for our wrong actions. We should repent even of wrong thoughts. *Repent* means more than just to say we are sorry and then keep on doing the same old thing. The word actually means "to turn." Christ is calling you to turn from sin and live according to His ways.

The Lord disciplines those He loves. When He sets a boundary, it is for your good. When He lets you stumble in order to show you the right path, this is for your very best. He has great plans for you, and in order to see those plans unfold in an amazing way, you must follow the ways of Jesus.

Lord, when You discipline me, help me to remember it is for my good. I repent now of sin and turn to You. Amen.

OBEY WHAT YOU READ IN THE BIBLE

*"See! I am coming soon. The one who obeys
what is written in this Book is happy!"*

REVELATION 22:7

Jesus is coming soon. We don't know the date or the hour. No one except the Father knows this information. People have guessed, predicted, and wondered. But no one knows when the Lord will return.

What we do know is that it is important to be ready at all times. Jesus says He will come as a thief in the night. Does anyone expect a robber who comes during the night? No! We are asleep at night, not sitting up ready and waiting for someone to break into our homes. What Jesus means is that we will not—we cannot—know the time of His second coming. So, we must always be prepared.

How can you be ready for the second coming of Christ? You can read the Bible and do what it says. These are not instructions from your parents, teachers, or pastor alone. These are instructions straight from the mouth of Jesus! Read them here in the book of Revelation. He is coming soon, and whoever obeys the Bible will be blessed.

Jesus, help me to obey Your Word that I might be
happy and blessed when You come again. Amen.

LOOK FOR JESUS' RETURN

He Who tells these things says, "Yes, I am
coming soon!" Let it be so. Come, Lord Jesus.
REVELATION 22:20

We should long for the second coming of Jesus. The writer of Revelation begs Jesus to come soon.

Even though we have many good things and many blessings in this life, the next life in heaven with the Lord will be wonderful beyond our wildest dreams. There will be no pain there, no crying, no fear. There will be no more death or disappointment. We will worship Him together with believers of every tribe and tongue. This means that in heaven there will be people from all over the world and from every culture, speaking different languages. We will have one thing in common—our love for Jesus Christ and our acceptance of Him as Lord and Savior.

Just as you long for Christmas morning and the presents you get to unwrap, pray that Jesus will return very soon. He promises to bring rewards for us according to what we have done.

Are you living out your life on earth doing God's will? Are you working for the kingdom of God? Do you spend time in His Word and in prayer? Do you serve Him by serving those in need? Your rewards in heaven will be great.

Lord Jesus, come quickly. I know life in heaven
will be much better than life here on earth. Amen.

MAKE THINGS RIGHT WITH OTHERS

*"Agree with the one who is against you while you are
talking together, or he might take you to court. The court
will hand you over to the police. You will be put in prison.
For sure, I tell you, you will not be let out of prison until
you have paid every piece of money of the fine."*

MATTHEW 5:25–26

The Lord wants us to make things right with others quickly. He explains here how complicated the process can get when people don't settle things outside of court. If two people are walking to court and can come to an agreement and settle their differences, that is best. Otherwise, the court may get the police involved, and someone may even end up in prison. Jesus always encouraged people to live at peace when at all possible. We should go to great lengths and take every chance we have to make things right with those around us.

This idea applies to kids as well as adults. Isn't it usually better to handle an argument without taking it to the teacher? Have you ever seen an issue grow bigger and bigger and the kids end up in the principal's office? This kind of scenario can be avoided if people just learn to get along. Make every effort to end anger that is not appropriate. Certainly, there is a time to disagree and even to be angry. But to the best of your ability, live at peace and seek to have peaceful relationships.

*Lord, show me where and when I need to make things
right with others. Help me to be quick to do so. Amen.*

LOVING THOSE WHO ARE HARD TO LOVE

"If you love those who love you, what reward can you expect from that? Do not even the tax-gatherers do that?"

MATTHEW 5:46

Have you ever been asked by a teacher to include a student in your group? Maybe it was on the playground, or maybe it was in the classroom when project groups were being formed. Has it ever been hard to say yes? Sometimes that child who can't find a group is difficult to work with or be around for a variety of reasons.

You might have good reason for not wanting to be around the other kid. In Jesus' day, people avoided tax collectors because they were hard to like. People didn't really want them in their group. Sometimes the dislike was understandable or even deserved by the tax collector. But that doesn't change the command of Jesus.

He calls us to love those who are not easy to love. He calls us to accept that other student in our group—not with a shrug but with a smile. Anyone can love their friends. It takes an individual changed by the grace of God to be kind to that hard-to-love student. Are you up for the challenge?

God, help me love the unlovable. Help me look
for good in all people because we have
all been made in Your image. Amen.

TURN THE OTHER CHEEK

"You have heard that it has been said, 'An eye for an eye and a tooth for a tooth.' But I tell you, do not fight with the man who wants to fight. Whoever hits you on the right side of the face, turn so he can hit the other side also."

MATTHEW 5:38–39

Jesus wants us to love one another and put the well-being of others before ourselves. We are not to seek revenge. We are not to fight back. We are not to be aggressive. We are to accept when someone is unfair to us, and we are to depend on God to be faithful to take care of us because we are His children.

What does this look like for a kid your age? It doesn't mean you stand there and let a bully pound on you. It does mean you don't take the chance to insult or injure someone who has hurt you. It means you let things go. Smile at that person who is mean to you. Don't plan a way to get back at them. Don't tattle just for the sake of getting the other person in trouble. Only tell when you really need to.

It also means living at peace. It means being the one who stops the fight or argument before it gets worse. It's hard for someone to argue with you if you are silent. It's hard for someone to keep fighting you if you refuse to participate.

Lord, help me to be a peacemaker
and turn the other cheek. Amen.

IN MY FATHER'S HOUSE

He said to them, "Why were you looking for Me?
Do you not know that I must be in My Father's house?"
They did not understand the things He said to them.
LUKE 2:49–50

If you have a parent who is a firefighter, chances are you have hung out at the fire station. If you're a teacher's kid, you may have seen the mysterious teachers' lounge! If your parent is a truck driver, you may have hit the open road with him in the summertime, sitting high above all the cars on the road, listening to the radio.

Kids hang out where their parents are. Jesus was missing, so why didn't Mary and Joseph know where to look? After all, the temple was His Father's house.

Jesus knew far more than the religious teachers. They marveled at His wisdom. They were shocked at His age. He was so young to be such a powerful teacher. He could explain scripture better than they could! He was, although this truth had not yet been shown to them, the Son of God.

Would your friends be surprised to find you at church? Reading your Bible? Hanging out with other Christians? Maybe spending spring break on a mission trip or summer break at a Bible camp? Make sure you are living in a manner worthy of your calling. No one should be shocked to find you in the house of the Lord.

God, may I be known as a Christ follower everywhere I go. Amen.

ARE YOU THROWING STONES?

Then He stood up and said, "Anyone of you who is
without sin can throw the first stone at her."

JOHN 8:7

Are you quick to call out others' sins? Do you gossip with friends about this person or that person and their bad choices? Do their rebellious ways shock you? Do you think they deserve to be punished? What if Jesus saw this person you are chatting about? What if Jesus were there? What if Jesus had the chance to decide the punishment?

Guess what? He does.

When a woman was caught in sin, the teachers of the law tried to trick Jesus. They tried to trap Him with words and laws. They wanted to see what He would say. They asked if they should stone the woman for her misbehavior according to the law of Moses. Jesus gave a wise answer. It was not the one they expected. It was beyond them. In fact, it was beyond this world. It dripped of grace and forgiveness. It smelled of freedom. It was a simple request that the person there in the crowd who had never sinned throw the first stone at her.

There was no one in the crowd who had never sinned, except for Jesus. No one threw a stone that day.

Stop throwing stones at school. Stop gossiping. Stop dealing out punishments you feel are deserved.

If Jesus shows grace, shouldn't we?

Lord, forgive me for throwing stones. Help me to reach out to those who don't know You and show them the way. Amen.

GOD OF THE IMPOSSIBLE

*Jesus looked at them and said, "This cannot be done
by men. But with God all things can be done."*

MATTHEW 19:26

The wonderful thing about God is that with Him all things are possible. When you look at a situation and think it is hopeless, it is not. When someone is so far from God that you think she could never come to know Him, she could. When you feel as if you can't go on, you can.

All things are possible with God.

An old song says, "God is so good." Another line of the song says, "God answers prayers." Great power is wrapped up in those words. God is so very good. He is also so very able. He can heal sicknesses and provide money and jobs and friends. He can even forgive sin and give a broken sinner eternal life.

There is great power in prayer. Prayer changes things. Prayer can impact the very heart of God. God hears your prayers. So when the circumstances seem impossible, remember that you serve a God who is able to do just that—the impossible. Pray and trust that God will always do what is best for us, whether we understand it or not.

God, You are so good, and You answer prayers. I love that
You are able to do more than I can even imagine. You are the
God of the impossible. Hear my requests now, even the ones
that seem impossible to me. Work in my life, I pray. Amen.

THE ALPHA AND THE OMEGA

The Lord God says, "I am the First and the Last, the beginning
and the end of all things. I am the All-powerful One
Who was and Who is and Who is to come."

REVELATION 1:8

One way to understand Jesus better and to know Him better is to
know the names He goes by. Many names are given to Jesus in the
Bible. He is called the Good Shepherd and the Son of God.

In Revelation, the very last book of the Bible, Jesus says that He
is the First and the Last. He calls Himself the Alpha and the Omega.
Alpha is the first letter of the Greek alphabet, and Omega is the last
letter. Jesus is saying He is the A and the Z.

Jesus has been alive forever. He has no beginning, and He will
have no end. Jesus Christ is forever and ever and ever. Because
Jesus died on the cross for us and we have been forgiven of our sins
through faith in Him, we will also live forever. We have been given
eternal life with Christ in heaven.

Jesus, You are the A and the Z, the beginning
and the end. I am thankful that I will spend
eternity in heaven with You. Amen.

POWER OVER DEATH AND HELL

"Do not be afraid. I am the First and the Last. I am the Living One. I was dead, but look, I am alive forever. I have power over death and hell."

REVELATION 1:17–18

The beautiful thing about Jesus' death is that we know the end of the story. Death, which is usually thought of as an ending, was only the beginning!

Jesus died for our sins, and when He rose again, many people saw Him. They saw with their own eyes the scars on His hands from the nails. They saw a man who was once dead now walking around alive and well. This was an "only God" type of situation. People saw His body broken and covered in blood on the cross. They saw His lifeless body taken down and buried in a tomb. They saw a gigantic stone rolled against the entrance.

And then they saw the dead man walking. They heard Him talking. He was truly the Son of God, risen again.

Jesus declares in the book of Revelation that He indeed has power over death and hell. He is the Almighty One, the beginning and the end. He is sovereign over all things.

Just when you feel that you have reached the end of your story, you may be on the edge of a new and exciting beginning. Look up! With Jesus, all things are possible. He even rose up from the dead. He can do a mighty work in your life.

Jesus, I am thankful that I know You, the one who has power over death and hell. Amen.

LOVE JESUS ALL OF YOUR LIFE

*"But I have this one thing against you.
You do not love Me as you did at first."*

REVELATION 2:4

When you first receive a great gift, you use it all the time, don't you? At first, that is. You just can't get enough of that brand-new video game or cool building set. But after some time passes, the newness wears off. A few parts go missing. And you find yourself wanting something different, something new.

The same is true of your Christian walk. It's exciting at first. You love Jesus. You want to tell others about Him. You learn Bible verses and pray. You can't get enough of Jesus. And then. . .the newness wears off. Distractions come.

This half-heartedness is part of sinful human nature. In Revelation 2, Jesus warned a group of believers to love Him as they did at first.

Stay the course. Love the Lord with all your heart, soul, and mind all your life. Look for fresh ways to worship Him. Find a new spot to read His Word daily. Get into a Bible study group. Memorize a new scripture verse. Run the race slow and steady, day by day, with Christ leading you.

Lord Jesus, empower me to love You all my days
and to love You with all my heart, I pray. Amen.

LOVE THE UNLOVABLE

"If you say hello only to the people you like, are you doing any more than others? The people who do not know God do that much."

MATTHEW 5:47

Loving those who love you is easy—it takes little to no effort. If Grandma hugs you and bakes cookies with you, she's easy to love. If a friend shares her best toys and games with you, loving her is simple. You are, in a sense, loving in return. You are giving back what you receive.

Where things get tricky is loving those who are not very lovable. That kid at school who acts better than everyone else. That bully who hurls insults at others. That kid who is just. . .different.

Loving these people requires more effort. Reaching out to such individuals doesn't come naturally. But reach out anyway!

Jesus calls us to love the unlovable. He even says to love our enemies. If we only love the grandmas and BFFs in our little worlds, who will reach the bullies? The snobs? Those who are just. . .different? Challenge yourself today to speak to someone you normally would ignore. Offer encouragement. Invite him to a party, or even just to sit next to you. Say hello. Smile. It's the way Jesus commands us to live.

Lord, give me the strength to love the unlovable.
Enable me to see the person who needs a friend,
and help me to be that friend. Amen.

DON'T BE A SHOW-OFF

*"Be sure you do not do good things in front
of others just to be seen by them. If you do,
you have no reward from your Father in heaven."*

MATTHEW 6:1

Do you have a sibling who acts one way when Mom is around and then a totally different way once her back is turned? Have you ever been guilty of this yourself? Sometimes we turn on good behavior when we know someone else is going to see us, especially a teacher or parent.

In the Bible, Jesus tells us not to do good in front of others just to be seen by them. In other words, when the offering plate is passed at church, we shouldn't make a big show of putting in our five-dollar bill. If you feel led to give some of your allowance money to God, do so quietly in a humble way. The point is not for your family and friends to see the amount you are giving and be impressed. In fact, this takes away from the meaning of the gift. God doesn't reward good deeds that we do in order to show off or look good.

Lord, help me do good things in order to please You and to help others. Remind me never to do good just so it can be seen by those around me. In Jesus' name I pray. Amen.

GOD SEES YOU

*"Your giving should be in secret. Then your
Father Who sees in secret will reward you."*

MATTHEW 6:4

Have you ever felt misunderstood? Maybe you tend to be shy. Did someone mistake this shyness for snobby behavior? Did someone think you were being rude when in fact you were just feeling overwhelmed so you didn't speak much?

This type of misunderstanding happens at times because others can't see your heart or mind. They see only the outward part of you and may misunderstand the feelings or attitudes behind your actions.

God does not misunderstand us. He sees our hearts. God is able to be in all places at all times. He hears many prayers at once. He sees beyond the outside to the emotions and motives of a person.

When you give to the Lord, whether it is a gift of your money, time, or abilities, give with a cheerful heart. Give quietly— not in a way that says, "Look at me! I am giving all of this to God! Am I great or what?"

Give in secret. Keep it quiet. Don't announce it or brag about it. Then God, who sees all the secret things, will reward you.

God, I want my giving to please You. I don't need the approval of others. I don't need them to be impressed with my offering. I give You my life—my time, my talents, and a portion of all the money I have. Use me as You will. I know my reward will be greater when I give with the right attitude. Amen.

FORGIVE OTHERS

"If you forgive people their sins, your Father in heaven will forgive your sins also. If you do not forgive people their sins, your Father will not forgive your sins."

MATTHEW 6:14–15

Jesus came to make a way of peace between sinners and a holy God. But that is not the only reason He came. He also taught that we should be at peace with one another. Over and over in the teachings of our Savior, we find an emphasis on reconciliation. To *reconcile* means to be brought back together, to restore a friendly relationship between two people or groups.

Forgiving others is important. If you find it hard to forgive someone who has hurt you, try praying for that individual. As you pray for God to bless him and ask for specific things you know this person needs, your heart will be softened. You will be much more able and ready to forgive after praying for him. You may have to pray for days or even weeks. Some hurts are deeper than others. God knows that you are hurt. He understands. But He does want you to try to be reconciled with the other person if at all possible.

God, help me to forgive the person who has hurt me. I pray for this person right now in this moment. I ask You to bless _____ (fill in the name). I ask You to soften my heart that I might be able to forgive _____ for hurting me. In Jesus' name. Amen.

WHAT IS FASTING ALL ABOUT?

*"When you go without food so you can pray better, put oil
on your head and wash your face. Then nobody
knows you are going without food. Then your
Father Who sees in secret will reward you."*

MATTHEW 6:17–18

Jesus taught that sometimes a person can pray better when she sets aside food for a time. This is called fasting. Sometimes a person will choose to fast in order to focus fully on God and a specific prayer need.

If you decide to fast in order to pray in a very special way, resist the temptation to make a big show of it. You wouldn't want to brag about fasting any more than you would want to brag about giving to God. It should be a private thing between you and your heavenly Father. He sees.

Setting aside one meal or more in order to spend that time fully bowed before God may lead you to deeper prayer. You may go past the surface to really seek God on the matter. This type of prayer touches the heart of God because He knows all things and He sees that you are truly wanting to know His will.

Fasting is one way to pray better. Be sure to spend some of your prayer time listening. Just sit quietly before the Lord. Don't do all the talking. Often, as you meditate on the words of scripture or simply sit before God, you will sense Him leading you.

God, please show me if there is a time I need to fast
in order to pray in a more focused way. Amen.

THE COST OF
FOLLOWING JESUS

A teacher of the Law came to Jesus. He said,
"Lord, I will follow You wherever You go." Jesus said
to him, "Foxes have holes. Birds have nests. But the
Son of Man has no place to lay His head."
MATTHEW 8:19–20

A man who came to Jesus and said he would follow Him anywhere had not counted the cost of such a statement. This means he had not thought about all he would have to give up, or sacrifice, in order to become a disciple of Jesus Christ.

Jesus told the man that foxes have holes and birds have nests. You may ask, *What does that have to do with anything?* Well, Jesus went on to explain that the Son of Man (Jesus) had no place to lay His head. In other words, Jesus did not have a home.

In order to follow Jesus, the man would have to give up everything. He would face homelessness and poverty. He would go without the finer things. He would travel and grow tired from long days of service and work.

Count the cost of following Jesus today. Are you willing to pay it? Will you sacrifice being popular? Will you risk being made fun of? Are you sure you want to miss out on some things because of Jesus? As you grow up, the sacrifices will be even greater. Count the cost. And then. . .take up your cross and follow Jesus. You will never regret that choice!

Lord, I choose to follow You at any cost. Amen.

JESUS CAME FOR SINNERS

The proud religious law-keepers saw this. They said to the followers
of Jesus, "Why does your Teacher eat with men who gather taxes
and with sinners?" Jesus heard them and said, "People who are
well do not need a doctor. But go and understand these words,
'I want loving-kindness and not a gift to be given.' For I have not
come to call good people. I have come to call those who are sinners."

MATTHEW 9:11–13

Jesus ate with tax collectors. This may not seem like a big deal until
you hear that the tax collectors were known for being dishonest. They
often took more money than they should have from the people. Why
would Jesus hang out with sinners?

Because that was why He came. That was His purpose.

Jesus died for all sins ever committed—past, present, and future.
Our only job is to come to Him and accept His free gift of salvation.
We should be the ones dying for our sins, but He took our sins upon
Himself.

Jesus would not have needed to come and die for us if we were
perfect. But we are all sinners. Ever since the garden of Eden when
Adam and Eve fell to the temptation of the first sin, people have been
separated from our holy God. The only way back to Him is through
Jesus. Remember that Jesus associated with sinners. We are no better
than the tax collectors. We sin every single day.

Thank You, Jesus, for coming to die for
the sins of all humankind. Amen.

HEALED IN AN INSTANT

She said to herself, "If I only touch the bottom of
His coat, I will be healed." Then Jesus turned around.
He saw her and said, "Daughter, take hope! Your faith
has healed you." At once the woman was healed.

MATTHEW 9:21–22

Don't miss these two words in this scripture: "at once." The woman was healed *at once* when she touched the hem of Jesus' robe. She was not admitted to a hospital for tests. She did not require surgery. She had lived with this blood disorder for many years, but in an instant, she was healed.

Jesus healed the sick. He made those who were lame walk again. Blind eyes were opened to see the world. Even better than this as He walked the dusty roads, town after town, He forgave sins. Often He would point out to the people that forgiveness of sins was even more important than physical healing. The forgiveness of sins, offered only by Almighty God, gave the person eternal life.

Have faith that in a moment's time, Jesus can heal. He may choose another route for you. He may choose to work through people or doctors or even your thoughts. But know that He is able to fully heal on the spot in one moment.

Jesus, thank You for healing the woman who was so in need
of a new life that day. Thank You also for the physical,
mental, and spiritual healing You offer us today. Amen.

ONLY JESUS

He said to them, "Go now! For the girl is not dead,
but is sleeping." But they laughed at Him. He sent the
people outside. Then He went in and took the girl's hand.
She was raised up. News of this went out into all the country.

MATTHEW 9:24–26

The people weren't wrong. The girl was not sleeping; she was dead. She had no pulse. She had no breath in her, no life. And then. . .

The girl lived again.

Only Jesus can do such a miracle. He brought the dead to life on more than one occasion. Remember Lazarus whom Jesus called out of the tomb after he had been dead for several days?

This girl was brought back to life, and there is no other explanation than the miraculous work of the Son of God.

The news went out to all the country, yet many still did not believe. Some said Jesus healed because He was demonic. Some simply could not see the miraculous works. Some feared they would lose their authority if they bowed to this one who did things they knew they could never do and never even explain!

Only Jesus.

The next time you need an "only Jesus" moment, look up. Say a prayer. Ask your miracle-working Savior to work a miracle in your life. He is still in the business today!

Jesus, thank You for doing miracles so many could
come to know You. Thank You for continuing to
display Your great, unmistakable power. Amen.

THE HOLY SPIRIT GIVES US WORDS TO SPEAK

"When you are put into their hands, do not worry what you will say or how you will say it. The words will be given you when the time comes. It will not be you who will speak the words. The Spirit of your Father will speak through you."
MATTHEW 10:19–20

Jesus told His disciples not to worry about what they would say because the Spirit of the Father would speak through them. The Holy Spirit is often known to provide just the right words for a believer to speak.

For example, if you are afraid to share the good news of Jesus, don't be! The Holy Spirit will go before you and will give you the right words. Sometimes a perfect scripture verse or example may come to mind to help make things clear for the person. That is not from you; that is from God.

Trust God not only in the big things—like to keep the universe turning! Trust Him in the little things. Ask Him to give you the right words to speak and to guide you when to speak. At times silence can be even more powerful than speaking. At times we are called to pray for someone for a long while before we ever speak a word directly to them.

If you are in trouble, turn to God. He will help you.

God is always near. He protects and comforts, and He even gives us words to speak.

Lord, show me when to speak and
give me the right words. Amen.

FAMILIES MAY BE DIVIDED OVER CHRISTIANITY

"A man will be hated by his own family."

MATTHEW 10:36

This verse of scripture on its own sounds horrible, doesn't it? Why would someone be hated by his family? Surely this is not from God! Yet it is.

This verse is found among others that speak of family members turning against one another and being divided over the issue of. . .Jesus.

What Jesus means here in this warning is that we must count the cost of following Him. Christians must realize that others may not like us when we are sold out for Jesus Christ. They may make fun of us, turn against us, or even hate us. Some people have come to Christ and become His followers at great cost, laying down their past lives completely. Their own families have disowned them.

Know that living a true Christian life won't always be easy. Jesus tells us that in the world we will have trouble, but He has overcome the world (John 16:33). Even if your own family turned against you, would you still follow Christ?

Lord, help me to follow You not just when it's easy,
but even if my loved ones were to turn against me. Amen.

LOVE JESUS MOST

*"He who loves his father and mother more than Me is
not good enough for Me. He who loves son or daughter
more than Me is not good enough for Me."*

MATTHEW 10:37

Jesus said to "love the Lord your God with all your heart and with
all your soul and with all your mind" (Matthew 22:37). So it should
come as no surprise when we hear Him say we shouldn't love anyone
more than we love Christ.

We must seek to put Jesus above all else in our lives. Certainly,
the Lord has put your parents in your life as authority figures. You
are to honor and obey them. One day when you are older, you might
fall in love and get married. You may become a parent. You should
love your spouse and children dearly. But still, no one should come
before Jesus Christ in your life—not your parents, siblings, best friend,
or anyone else.

The person who has Christ in the driver's seat of his life has the
right priorities. Everything else will fall into place if you have Jesus
as number one!

Lord, help me to always keep You first in my life.
I want You to be number one. I want to love You
more than anyone or anything else. Amen.

REST IN JESUS

*"Follow My teachings and learn from Me. I am gentle and
do not have pride. You will have rest for your souls."*

MATTHEW 11:29

Rest is found in Christ alone. This verse speaks of it. Certainly, Jesus doesn't mean we should sit around in an eternal state of rest. Far from it! He calls us to do good deeds, to love and serve others, and to share the gospel. But His teachings and commands, while they may bring about hardship in life, bring great joy. The life centered around Christ is the life of peace.

You can come to Christ with your worries, your sins, your burdens—the things that weigh you down. Are you afraid of something or someone? Take this to Jesus. Are you concerned about the future? Give it to Him. Lay your cares at His feet because He asks you to. He calls you, but you must answer. Every single day, we should come before Jesus and empty ourselves of self, refreshing ourselves with Christ.

Find rest—the only true rest—in Jesus.

Lord, take my burdens and worries.
Replace them with rest, please. Amen.

TREES AND FRUIT MUST MATCH

"A good tree gives good fruit. A bad tree gives bad fruit. A tree is known by its fruit."

MATTHEW 12:33

In Matthew 12:24, Christ was being accused of casting out demons. The verse says, "But when the proud religious law-keepers heard it, they said, 'This Man puts out demons only by Satan, the leader of demons.'"

Jesus' response to their accusation makes complete sense, and it can also be applied to our lives as Christ followers today.

Jesus basically said that if they were accusing Him of casting out demons (a good act) in the name of Satan (the evil one), then it was a bad thing. In other words, it didn't make sense.

Jesus used the example of a tree. How could a bad tree give good fruit? If he was of Satan, how could He cast demons out of a human being—such a miraculous good act?

Just as Jesus spoke of Himself, make sure that "your fruit matches your tree." We will all make mistakes, but seek to bear good fruit!

Lord, because You have made me righteous through
Your death on the cross, may I live a righteous
life that is holy and pleasing to You. Amen.

DON'T DOUBT

*At once Jesus put out His hand and took hold of him. Jesus
said to Peter, "You have so little faith! Why did you doubt?"*

MATTHEW 14:31

Peter doubted when he looked down and saw that he was walking on
water! It was pretty unbelievable, wouldn't you say? Before we shake
our heads in disapproval, we must realize that he was witnessing
a miracle. People can't walk on the surface of a body of water. And
yet. . .he was!

At the moment Peter looked down, he began to doubt and he
also began to sink! We can learn a lot from this story.

Peter knew Jesus. He had seen Him do other miracles such as
heal the sick. He had every reason to trust in the Lord, yet he didn't.
He took his eyes off the Son of God, and he began to go under. He
began to sink!

Our Savior is pleased when we rely on Him and put our trust in
Him. Consider all the times the Lord has shown up for you in your
life. Now, why would He stop showing up?

The next time you start to lose faith, look to Jesus. Bring to your
mind all the reasons you have to trust Him. Keep your eyes on Him.
Be confident in His faithfulness and in His ability to do miracles
even today.

Lord, help me remember that You are always with me and that
You can always be trusted. Increase my faith, I ask. Amen.

BE A GIVER

Jesus said to them, "How many loaves of bread do you have?" They said, "Seven loaves and a few small fish."

MATTHEW 15:34

What do you have? Are you an artist? Can you sing? Do you play an instrument? Can you ride a bike? Play a sport? Dance?

What do you own? Do you have a wagon? Some money in your piggy bank? Some extra food in the pantry at your house?

Whatever you have to offer, Jesus will make more of it. One kid on a hillside gave Jesus a little lunch of bread and fish. Jesus fed thousands with it, and afterward there were baskets and baskets full of leftovers.

Never think that because you are young, your gift is worthless. No one else handed over a lunch that day. Maybe it was the only one there, or maybe someone else was holding out. Maybe someone had a small amount of food tucked away in her pocket. Just enough for a snack. . .just enough for one person.

Imagine how that person must have felt on the walk home, especially compared to the boy who shared his lunch. Imagine missing the blessing of being a giver.

You will never regret giving all that you have to your Savior. Little is much when the Lord is in it.

Jesus, give me a cheerful heart that
loves to give to Your kingdom. Amen.

STAY AWAY FROM
FALSE TEACHERS

*"Why is it that you do not see that I was not talking to you about
bread? I was talking to you about keeping away from the yeast
of the proud religious law-keepers and the religious group of
people who believe no one will be raised from the dead."*

MATTHEW 16:11

Be careful to stay away from the teachings of those who don't believe
in Jesus. These teachings are all around you.

You will hear people say that Jesus is only one way of many, that
all gods are the same, and that it is a person's works that determine whether he goes to heaven.

But you know that Jesus said, "I am the Way and the Truth and the
Life. No one can go to the Father except by Me" (John 14:6).

You will hear teachers say that God will give you riches and wealth
if you just ask for them. But you know this is not right because you
have learned this truth: "First of all, look for the holy nation of God.
Be right with Him. All these other things will be given to you also"
(Matthew 6:33).

The "truth test" is this: Does the teaching line up with the Bible?
Does it ring true with scripture?

If you feel disturbed because you just aren't sure that what you
are hearing is the truth, that is the Holy Spirit within you. Now that
you are a Christian, you have been given an understanding that
many do not have. Listen to that still, small voice!

Lord, please help me be able to easily tell the
difference between true and false teachings. Amen.

THE PARABLE OF THE MAN WHO PLANTED SEEDS

*Jesus taught them many things by using picture-stories. He said,
"A man went out to plant seeds. As he planted the seeds, some fell
by the side of the road. The birds came and ate the seeds. Some
seeds fell between rocks. The seeds came up at once because there
was so little ground. When the sun was high in the sky, they dried up
and died because they had no root. Some seeds fell among thorns.
The thorns grew and did not give the seeds room to grow. Some
seeds fell on good ground and gave much grain. Some gave one
hundred times as much grain. Some gave sixty times as much grain.
Some gave thirty times as much grain. You have ears, then listen."*

MATTHEW 13:3–9

The seed that is planted in this picture-story is the Word of God.
The man who plants the seed is Jesus, perhaps along with some of
His ministers. The hearts of people are represented by four different types of soil. Will you be a hearer of the Word of God who is
easily robbed of the Word by Satan? Will you be careless? Will you
be a hearer who starts off right but has no true change of heart?
Will thorns—worldly things—distract you? Hebrews 6:8 tell us that
worldly things will be burned up one day. They are not lasting like
the Word of God. A true Christian allows the Word of the Lord to take
root and grow. She produces fruit for the kingdom.

Lord, help me be one who hears the Word
and lets it take root in my life. Amen.

113

JESUS TAUGHT WITH PARABLES

Jesus taught them many things by using picture-stories.

MATTHEW 13:3

Jesus often taught using stories, or parables. Most of us like to hear stories. Why? They allow us to use our imagination and create the picture in our mind. They also are easy to learn from, aren't they? Do you have a parent or grandparent who uses stories from his past in order to teach you valuable lessons?

Jesus used stories for a couple of reasons in His teaching. One reason was so that those who wanted to learn could understand His lessons better.

As you listen to or read the "picture-stories," or parables, found in the Bible, be open to what Jesus is trying to teach you through them. Pray for the Lord to give you understanding. Then be prepared to make the changes that the story may call for in your life. These stories were not told for entertainment purposes or just to be enjoyed. They were told so that believers might see the right ways to live. Apply the truths you learn from Jesus' stories, and you will experience great life change.

Lord, thank You for the stories You share with me
that help me understand how to live. Amen.

WHY JESUS TAUGHT WITH PICTURE-STORIES

*"This is why I speak to them in picture-stories.
They have eyes but they do not see. They have ears
but they do not hear and they do not understand."*

MATTHEW 13:13

Jesus spoke to large crowds. Not everyone there was truly interested in hearing what Jesus had to say and learning from it. Some were there just to see a miracle. They had heard of the signs and wonders Jesus performed. They wanted a show. They were not interested in His message. Some were there to try to trap Him by catching Him saying something wrong. They were power hungry, and they didn't want other people to follow Jesus.

Some people in the crowds truly were there to hear the words Jesus spoke. They loved His messages. They turned from sin and followed Jesus. They wanted to know how they should change and how to live according to God's ways. These are the people who understood the parables. Jesus gave these people the ability to understand. He wanted them to know the mysteries of God. The others were kept from understanding. This allowed Christ more time to teach and preach. If those who were against Jesus had understood the parables, He might have been arrested and His ministry would have ended sooner than God desired. Jesus was wise to teach in picture-stories, wasn't He?

Lord, help me always be one who seeks You and
tries to understand Your way for my life. Amen.

A SOFT HEART AND AN OPEN MIND

"The hearts of these people have become fat. They hear very little with their ears. They have closed their eyes. If they did not do this, they would see with their eyes and hear with their ears and understand with their hearts. Then they would be changed in their ways, and I would heal them."

MATTHEW 13:15

Some people have hardened their hearts toward God. They have stopped listening to God. They don't want to hear what He has to say, and they don't want to do what He asks them to do. Ephesians 4:18 describes it this way: "Their minds are in darkness. They are strangers to the life of God. This is because they have closed their minds to Him and have turned their hearts away from Him."

The opposite of a hardened heart is a soft heart, one that is ready to listen and learn from God. When you have a soft heart, you are willing to change the way you think about things so you can think like Jesus does about those things. A soft heart causes you to want to live as Jesus wants you to live.

If you have a soft heart, you can be convicted of sin. This means you can begin to see that you have been doing something wrong. You are eager to learn new things and make necessary changes.

In order to understand the stories Jesus told and to learn from them, keep an open mind and a humble heart.

Jesus, please open my mind and soften my heart
so that I might "get" the messages You have
for me in the parables You told. Amen.

UNDERSTAND AND OBEY THE LESSONS OF CHRIST

*Obey the Word of God. If you hear only and do not act,
you are only fooling yourself. Anyone who hears the Word
of God and does not obey is like a man looking at his face
in a mirror. After he sees himself and goes away, he forgets
what he looks like. But the one who keeps looking into God's
perfect Law and does not forget it will do what it says and
be happy as he does it. God's Word makes men free.*

JAMES 1:22–25

When you read the parables and discover their truths, apply them. Don't hear the message, understand it, and then just go on living as you did before. That would be silly!

The book of James in the Bible tells us this would be like a person who looks in the mirror and sees his face but then walks away and forgets what he looks like.

Look into the Word. Study it. Pray for God to reveal His truth to you. Then remember it. Put it into practice. God's Word will set you free.

Help me, Jesus, not just to read the parables
You shared but to understand them and put
them into practice in my life. Amen.

THE MUSTARD SEED

Jesus told them another picture-story. He said, "The holy nation of heaven is like mustard seed which a man planted in his field. It is the smallest of seeds. But when it is full-grown, it is larger than the grain of the fields and it becomes a tree. The birds of the sky come and stay in its branches."

MATTHEW 13:31–32

Have you ever planted a seed and watched a plant sprout and grow from it? God makes *huge* plants grow out of even tiny seeds, such as an acorn or a mustard seed. Those trees do great things—they provide shade and even homes for animals such as birds and squirrels.

The kingdom of heaven started off very tiny, with just a few people believing in Jesus, and then it grew—much like a tree—and now millions of people worldwide have trusted in Jesus as their personal Savior!

Right now, you are young. But don't let that discourage you. God can take even a small act and bring great things from it. He can grow and multiply it. All you have to do is trust Him to do that work. You may be wondering what small things you could do. Well, you could do chores at home to help your parents without even having to be asked. You could say hello to other kids in the halls at school or invite them to sit with you if they are alone. You could bow to pray over your food even if no one else is.

God, even though I'm young, I can
make a difference. Show me how! Amen.

THE PICTURE-STORY
OF THE YEAST

Jesus gave them another picture-story. He said, "The holy nation of heaven is like yeast that a woman put into three pails of flour until it had become much more than at first."

MATTHEW 13:33

In this parable, the flour is used to represent the world and all those living in it, and the yeast represents the Christians. When someone bakes bread, the yeast is the ingredient that causes it to rise. It only takes a small amount of yeast to make bread fluffy and yummy. In the parable of the yeast, Jesus shows us that it only takes a few Christians to make a big difference in the world. In Matthew 28:19–20, Christ commands us to go into the world and tell people everywhere how much Jesus loves them. In this way, we are like a little bit of yeast, making a whole loaf of bread wonderfully delicious. So who can we share the good news of Jesus with? Classmates, teachers, neighborhood friends, the cashier at the grocery store. . .anyone!

As citizens of the kingdom of heaven, we pray for those who don't believe in Jesus. We do things to show that we love Jesus. And we share with everyone around us that Jesus Christ is the King, the Savior of the world, and the Messiah.

Lord, I pray for those who do not yet know You. I also ask that You will give me opportunities to show Your love and share the good news of Jesus. Amen.

THE PARABLE OF THE TREASURE BURIED IN THE FIELD

"The holy nation of heaven is like a box of riches buried in a field. A man found it and then hid it again. In his joy he goes and sells all that he has and buys that field."

MATTHEW 13:44

In this picture-story told by Jesus, we read about a man who found the kingdom of heaven although he wasn't looking for it. Jesus calls everyone, not just those who are actively looking for Him. Some people are against Christ or don't even know they need to be saved when someone shares the Good News with them. Then they come to know Christ as their Savior.

When the man found the kingdom of heaven, he hid it and went and sold all that he owned in order that he might have it. Can you imagine selling everything you own? The kingdom of heaven was worth a lot to the man. Can we buy our way into heaven? No! We are saved by God's grace when we believe in Jesus. We can't earn or brag about salvation. It is a gift.

From this picture-story, we learn that Jesus is calling even those who want nothing to do with Him. Think about Saul who met the Lord on the road to Damascus and was forever changed! He was changed so much that he was given a new name: Paul. He traded a life of persecuting Christians for a life of preaching Christ to anyone who would listen. We also learn that a life with Christ is worth everything—absolutely everything.

Jesus, thank You for picture-stories.
I love learning from You. Amen.

THE PARABLE OF
THE PEARL

"Again, the holy nation of heaven is like a man who buys and sells. He is looking for good pearls. When he finds one good pearl worth much money, he goes and sells all that he has and buys it."
MATTHEW 13:45–46

The man in this parable was looking. He was on the lookout for Jesus, unlike the man in the parable of the treasure buried in the field. He was searching.

A lot of people in this world are searching for something to fill up the emptiness they feel inside. If you have found Christ, you are blessed to be one who knows that only Jesus can fill up that spot in our lives. Some have said there is a Christ-shaped hole in all of us that can be filled only by Him.

In both this parable and the one before it, the man is said to give up everything in order to have the kingdom of God. So what does this mean, since we know salvation is a free gift? Christ Himself said that a person must count the cost. He wants us to know up front that we may experience hard times when people make fun of us or treat us wrongly. Jesus must be more important to us than anything—video games, sports, friendships, even family. We are called to make our relationship with Christ the most important one in our lives.

God, I want my relationship with You to be number one in my life. Help me to see where I need to reprioritize. Amen.

GOOD NEWS AND BAD NEWS

*"The holy nation of heaven is like a big net which was let down
into the sea. It gathered fish of every kind. When it was full, they
took it to the shore. They sat down and put the good fish into pails.
They threw the bad fish away. It will be like this in the end of the
world. Angels will come and take the sinful people from among
those who are right with God. They will put the sinful people into a
stove of fire where there will be loud crying and grinding of teeth."*

MATTHEW 13:47–50

This picture-story is good news for some and bad news for others.
At the end of the world, those who follow Christ will go to heaven.
Those who have rejected Jesus will face a very different eternity. They
will be cast into hell for a horrible existence.

Part of being a citizen of the kingdom of heaven is sharing the
gospel with others so that they don't get thrown away like the "bad
fish" in this picture-story. We simply must share the good news that
was shared with us. We cannot keep it to ourselves. Some people
may accept the news you share. They may call on Jesus to save them.
Others will reject the truth. That is their choice, but in the end it will
cost them dearly—it will cost them eternity, where they will live forever separated from God.

Jesus, thank You for saving me. Help me tell others
about You so that they might go to heaven also. Amen.

THE SECOND COMING

"Now learn something from the fig tree. When the branch begins to grow and puts out its leaves, you know summer is near. In the same way, when you see all these things happen, you know the Son of Man is near. He is even at the door. For sure, I tell you, the people of this day will not pass away before all these things have happened."

MARK 13:28–30

No one knows when Jesus will return. The Bible says only God knows this information. But there are signs that will tell us the second coming is near.

We need to live life in such a way that if Christ returned today, we would be ready. We need to live ready! So how do we do this? Well, we live according to what God has taught us in His Word.

We live a life full of prayer, reading and studying scripture, loving others, giving, and sharing the gospel boldly with those around us. We don't put these things off for another time. Maybe you are waiting for a less busy season. But one will not come. Every season will have its own reasons to put off living the way we should, so begin today! Carve out the time that it takes to seek Jesus and to live for Him. It is a commitment. Remember, Christ tells us to count the cost before we "sign up" for the Christian life.

Live ready! Live in such a way that if Jesus' second coming happens sooner than you expect, you are ready for His return.

Jesus, help me to live in such a way that I
will be ready when You come again. Amen.

THE POWER OF THE HOLY SPIRIT

He said, "How can the devil put out the devil? A nation cannot last if it is divided against itself. A family cannot last if it is divided against itself. If the devil fights against himself and is divided, he cannot last. He will come to an end. No man can go into a strong man's house and take away his things, unless he ties up the strong man first. Only then can he take things from his house. For sure, I tell you, all sins will be forgiven people, and bad things they speak against God. But if anyone speaks bad things against the Holy Spirit, he will never be forgiven. He is guilty of a sin that lasts forever."

MARK 3:23–29

The scribes were against Jesus. They wanted to persuade people that Christ was casting out demons through Satan's power. In this picture-story about the strong man, Jesus explained that if He were casting out demons through Satan's power, then Satan would be working against himself.

The strong man is Satan, the house is his domain, and the goods are his possessions. In order to bind Satan, Jesus would have had to use a different, stronger power. He used the power of the Holy Spirit.

Jesus warned of eternal punishment for those who were accusing Him of using Satan's power here. In doing so, they were blaspheming the Holy Spirit.

Jesus, I am thankful I have You, a Savior whose power is so much stronger than that of the evil one, Satan. Amen.

WHAT DID JESUS TEACH ABOUT SIN AND SALVATION?

*He said, "The time has come. The holy nation
of God is near. Be sorry for your sins, turn from
them, and believe the Good News."*

MARK 1:15

Jesus preached that people should be sorry for their sins, turn from them, and believe the good news. There are three steps here. Be careful not to miss any of them.

The first step is to be sorry for sin. Being sorry is a feeling. It can overwhelm us at times. When we realize that Christ died for our sins, not His own, we feel sad. We recognize that God is holy and we, just like our ancestors Adam and Eve, have fallen short of His perfection through sin. That's a tough truth to swallow. It leads us to feel sorry.

The next step is an important one. To repent means literally to turn. Turn from your sin and back to God. In other words, make a change in your life based on the sorrow you feel for having sinned. Repent.

The third step is to believe the good news. Accept Christ as your Savior. His salvation is a free gift—no strings attached. Believe in the Lord Jesus Christ, and you will be saved.

I am sorry for my sin, God, and I repent and
turn from it. I believe the good news of Jesus.
I am so thankful He is my Savior. Amen.

THEY LAID DOWN THEIR NETS

*Jesus said to them, "Follow Me. I will make you fish
for men!" At once they left their nets and followed Him.*

MARK 1:17–18

Jesus called fishermen to follow Him. The Bible says they left their nets and followed Him. This was a big deal!

They laid down their jobs. Those nets were the way the fishermen made money. They were the way they paid the bills. Their actions would have been like a business professional tossing his computer in the garbage—the computer that contained all the files and documents necessary to perform his job. It would have been like a doctor walking out of his office with Jesus or a taxi cab driver opening the door of his taxi and walking off with Jesus, never to return.

When Jesus calls you to do something, do you follow quickly? Do you stand around counting the cost, or are you like the fishermen who became disciples that day? Do you leave everything behind in order to follow Christ?

What if you are called to do something for Jesus that will cost you your popularity or reputation? Will you think long and hard, or will the choice be a simple one?

Christ Jesus, may I be quick to follow Your call
in my life regardless of the cost. Amen.

JESUS IS STRONGER

*There was a man in the Jewish place of worship who had a
demon. The demon cried out, "What do You want of us, Jesus of
Nazareth? Have You come to destroy us? I know Who You are. You
are the Holy One of God." Jesus spoke sharp words to the demon
and said, "Do not talk! Come out of the man!" The demon threw
the man down and gave a loud cry. Then he came out of him.*

MARK 1:23–26

In these verses, Jesus commanded the demon to come out of the man,
and it threw the man down, gave a loud cry, and came out of him.

Jesus is more powerful than Satan and all his demons. One day,
every knee will bow and every tongue will call Jesus "King." For now,
Satan has some power, but in the end he will be defeated.

Know that Jesus is able to help you when Satan tempts you. When
Satan wishes for you to be afraid, Jesus stands ready to comfort and
give you courage. Jesus is the King of kings and the Lord of lords. He is
the Light of the World, while Satan is the prince of darkness. Jesus is
good. Satan is evil. Call upon your Savior, and He will come running.
He will protect you from the evil one.

Jesus, I pray that You will protect me from the
power of Satan. I know You are stronger. Amen.

NEAR TO JESUS

[Jesus] said to [the man healed of leprosy], "Tell no one about this. Go and let the religious leader of the Jews see you. Give the gifts Moses has told you to give when a man is healed of a disease. Let the leaders know you have been healed." But the man went out and talked about it everywhere. After this Jesus could not go to any town if people knew He was there. He had to stay in the desert. People came to Him from everywhere.

MARK 1:44–45

Jesus healed a man of leprosy and then instructed him to tell no one, but he did. Because he did, the crowds that came to hear and see Jesus grew. They were so large that Jesus could not go into any town if people heard He was coming. The streets would not hold the crowds.

We don't know why the man disobeyed and told of his healing. Perhaps he just couldn't contain the good news that he had been healed of the horrible disease. Whatever the reason, his actions increased the number of those who wanted to get near to Jesus.

At that time, Jesus could be in only one place at a time. He was in His human form. Now He has sent the Comforter, the Holy Spirit. All believers can be near to Jesus at the same time!

Thank You, Lord, that I can be near You and that
You hear and answer my prayers. Amen.

JESUS CALLS SINNERS

*He walked farther and saw Levi (Matthew) the son of
Alphaeus. Levi was sitting at his work gathering taxes.
Jesus said to him, "Follow Me." Levi got up and followed Him.*

MARK 2:14

Like the "wee little man Zaccheus" whom we know about from the
children's song, Levi collected taxes from the people. Tax collectors
were not popular with the people in Jesus' day. They were often
disliked and distrusted by members of the community.

Jesus called Levi, and he not only went with Jesus but later hosted
a banquet in his home. Jesus was there, along with many sinners.
When Jesus was questioned for eating with sinners, He gave His
well-known answer that He had not come for the healthy but for
the sick. He had come for those who were not right with God—those
who needed spiritual healing.

If Jesus chose to use a tax collector and to fellowship with sinners,
could He use someone who is poor? Someone who has been abused or
neglected? Someone who has done something really bad? Someone
who is far from God but who turns from sin and follows Him? You
bet! Jesus can use anyone—even you!

Jesus, thank You that despite what I may have done or
what may have been done to me, You can use me. Amen.

WHEAT AND WEEDS

"The servants of the man who planted the seed came and said to him, 'Sir, did you not plant good seed in your field? Why does it have weeds also?' The man who planted the seed said, 'Someone who hates me has done this.' The servants asked him, 'Should we go and pull the weeds out from among the good grain?' He said, 'No, because if you pull out the weeds, the good grain will come up also.'"

Jesus shared this story of a man who planted some wheat seeds in his field. His enemy came and planted some weed seeds among the wheat ones. As they grew, the farmers' servants asked the farmer if they should pull up the weeds. The farmer said not to pull them up because some of the good wheat might accidentally be uprooted if they did. The farmer let the wheat and the weeds grow alongside one another—mixed together until harvesttime. When the wheat was then collected to be used, the weeds were plucked up and burned.

From this picture-story, we learn that God allows believers and unbelievers to live together on this earth. At times, Christians may look at the lives of non-Christians and see them getting away with sinful lifestyles. In the end, unbelievers will receive their fair judgment. Right now it may even be hard to tell wheat from weeds—believers from unbelievers.

Lord, may my life easily be seen to be wheat, not weeds. Amen.

FORGIVENESS

"Then the king called for the first one. He said, 'You bad servant!
I forgave you. I said that you would not have to pay back any of
the money you owed me because you asked me. Should you not
have had pity on the other servant, even as I had pity on you?'
The king was very angry. He handed him over to men who would
beat and hurt him until he paid all the money he owed."

MATTHEW 18:32–34

Jesus told this parable about a king who asked his servants to pay back what they owed him. One particular servant owed a large sum of money, but he wasn't able to pay any of his debt. The king demanded that this man and his family be sold in order to pay the debt. When the servant begged him not to do so, the king listened and forgave the large debt. That same servant turned around and refused to show mercy to his own worker, who owed him much less money. When the king found out what his servant had done, he punished him severely.

Jesus used this parable to teach His followers that if we want God to forgive our sins, we must forgive others' sins against us.

Lord, help me forgive others for their sins against me so
that You might also forgive my sins against You. Amen.

THE GOOD SAMARITAN

"Which of these three do you think was a neighbor to the man who was beaten by the robbers?" The man who knew the Law said, "The one who showed loving-pity on him." Then Jesus said, "Go and do the same."

LUKE 10:36–37

Have you ever repotted a plant? Sometimes a plant must be moved from a small pot to a larger one so that it can survive. Repotting a plant involves getting your hands dirty. You have to dig in and do the work. But it's always worth it to see that plant flourishing in its new "home."

The parable of the good Samaritan shows us that God wants Christians to be kind to all human beings, regardless of their race, status, or physical traits. True kindness is often demonstrated by doing jobs that most people don't want to do.

In this parable, a Samaritan, a person often shunned by Jews, was the one who showed mercy to the injured man and took care of him. The priest and the Levite, who passed by the man, were known to preach about kindness, but the Samaritan was the one who *showed* it. Jesus tells us to do the same. Don't be afraid to get your hands dirty. The best way to show kindness is to help others even when it is inconvenient or difficult to do so.

Lord, help me be willing to show kindness to others even when it is not convenient or easy. Amen.

THE MISSING SHEEP

*Then Jesus told them a picture-story, saying, "What if one
of you had one hundred sheep and you lost one of them?
Would you not leave the ninety-nine in the country and go
back and look for the one which was lost until you find it?"*

LUKE 15:3–4

Imagine every desk in the classroom had a bag of small candies on
it, but then the teacher said one large candy was hidden in the room.
The students would go hunt for that hidden candy, right? They would
want to locate the one that was missing, of course!

Jesus told this parable—which is about sheep, not candy—to a
group of Pharisees and teachers who said it was wrong for Him to
spend time with sinners. Jesus told them that, of course, they would
go look for one missing sheep out of one hundred and rejoice when
it was located. After He shared this picture-story with His audience,
they were shocked.

Jesus went on to say, "I tell you, there will be more joy in heaven
because of one sinner who is sorry for his sins and turns from them,
than for ninety-nine people right with God who do not have sins to
be sorry for" (verse 7).

Lord, help me lead others to You so that they may be saved and
You might rejoice over lost souls coming to salvation. Amen.

THE PRODIGAL SON

"The son said to him, 'Father, I have sinned against heaven and against you. I am not good enough to be called your son.' But the father said to the workmen he owned, 'Hurry! Get the best coat and put it on him. Put a ring on his hand and shoes on his feet. Bring the calf that is fat and kill it. Let us eat and be glad. For my son was dead and now he is alive again. He was lost and now he is found. Let us eat and have a good time.'"

LUKE 15:21–24

The parable Jesus told of the prodigal son is a story of a man who takes his father's inheritance and wastes it all. He ends up so poor that he is forced to take a job feeding pigs for a living and eating their slop. The son returns to his father's house and begs to become just a servant there, knowing he no longer deserves to be a son. But the father runs to him and welcomes him with open arms, forgiving him and accepting him as his son once more.

God rejoices when we repent too! When we turn from sin and go back to God, He is always there waiting. No sin is too large for God to forgive. Is there a sin you need to ask God to forgive you of right now?

Lord, forgive me for _____ (insert the details here). I am honored and grateful to be called Your child. Amen.

THE PARABLE OF
THE TALENTS

*Jesus said, "I tell you, he who has, to him will
be given more. To him who does not have,
even the little he has will be taken from him."*

LUKE 19:26

The picture-story of the talents is about a man who entrusts his servants with his property while he goes away and travels. Before he leaves, he gives each servant a different sum of money. When he comes back, the man finds that all but one worked and made a profit from what he had given them. One wicked servant just hid the money.

God has blessed each one of us with different talents and gifts. Our duty is to use them to help other people and bring glory to our Creator God. Some people prefer to keep those gifts for themselves or are scared to use their gifts, like the servant who buried the money. If we don't use our talents and abilities for the Lord, they are useless.

What abilities have you been given? What are you blessed with? Do you sing or dance? Are you a good leader? Do you play a sport well? Are you organized? Maybe you are a writer. Maybe you have a wonderful speaking voice. Perhaps you are an expert when it comes to cars or machinery. Whatever your talents are, true joy comes when you find ways to use them in order to glorify and honor the Lord.

God, help me identify and use my gifts
and abilities for Your glory. Amen.

A FOUND COIN

"What if a woman has ten silver pieces of money and loses one of them? Does she not light a lamp and sweep the floor and look until she finds it? When she finds it, she calls her friends and neighbors together. She says to them, 'Be happy with me. I have found the piece of money I had lost.' I tell you, it is the same way among the angels of God. If one sinner is sorry for his sins and turns from them, the angels are very happy."

LUKE 15:8–10

Have you ever lost something valuable or an item that meant a lot to you? When you finally locate it, aren't you relieved and excited?

Jesus told a parable of a woman who had ten silver pieces of money and lost one of them. She searched high and low. Eventually she found it, and when she did, she was thrilled. Jesus used this story to explain how God's angels rejoice when even just one sinner repents and turns to God.

There is something else to be learned from this picture-story. What did the woman do when she lost the coin? She lit a lamp and swept the floor until she found it. This shows us that as believers, we should be searching high and low for those who are lost. When we find them, we should share Jesus with them so that they may be saved.

Lord, please give me a desire to lead the lost to You. Amen.

THE PARABLE OF THE GREAT SUPPER, PART 1

Then Jesus said to the leader of the proud religious law-keepers,
"There was a man who was giving a big supper. He asked
many people to come to eat. When it was about time to eat,
he sent one of the servants he owned to tell those he had
asked, saying, 'Come, everything is ready now.'"

LUKE 14:16–17

Imagine throwing the best party ever! What would it be like? Would you have balloons and streamers? An inflatable obstacle course? Would there be pizza? What kind of cake would you serve?

In the parable of the great supper, a man plans an amazing banquet, and yet his friends use ridiculous excuses not to come. The party host represents Jesus. The group of people who were invited represent the Jewish leaders of that day. The Pharisees rejected Christ as the way to God. They made excuses and turned down their opportunity to spend eternity in heaven with Christ.

Why in the world would they do this? The Pharisees should have gladly accepted salvation through Jesus, but they didn't want to come to God through Jesus. They wanted to come to God through the following of rules. They had made up many, many rules in addition to God's law for the people. They wanted to come to God through their own goodness, but that would never be acceptable to God.

Jesus, I am so thankful that You are the way,
the truth, and the life. I know I could never
come to God except through You. Amen.

THE PARABLE OF THE GREAT SUPPER, PART 2 (EXCUSES)

"They all gave different reasons why they could not come. The first said, 'I have bought some land and I must go and see it. Do not expect me to come.' Another one said, 'I have bought ten cows to use for working in my fields. I must go and try them out. Do not expect me to come.' And another one said, 'I have just been married and I cannot come.'"

LUKE 14:18–20

In Jesus' parable of the great supper, some of the excuses are lies. In Jesus' day nobody would have bought land or oxen without thoroughly checking out these purchases first. Being married was a true responsibility. But the married man had accepted the invitation previously. That meant he was duty-bound to attend, yet he decided to ignore his invitation.

People still make excuses today for rejecting Christ. Some desire money or possessions more than they wish to accept the invitation of Jesus to follow Him. Others get so busy with friends, video games, sports, and other activities that they won't make time for Jesus as their Lord and Savior. Many have responsibilities like school or work, but these duties should never be an excuse to say no to God. When Christ invites us to follow and serve Him, our answer should be "yes." He will empower us to obey and serve Him. Excuses only block us from His blessings.

Lord, help me to live a life that is free of making excuses. I want to obey whatever You lead me to do. Amen.

THE PARABLE OF THE GREAT SUPPER, PART 3

*"The servant came back and said, 'Sir, what you told
me to do has been done. But there are still some empty
places.' Then the owner said to his servant, 'Go out along
the roads leading away from the city and into the fields.
Tell them they must come. Do this so my house will be filled.
I tell you, not one of those I had asked will eat of my supper.'"*

LUKE 14:22–24

When the Pharisees rejected Jesus, He turned to the outcasts of that day—the poor, diseased, lame, and blind. In Bible times, these people were not treated well. The Pharisees thought such people could never be good enough, or righteous, in God's eyes.

The last group of people (those by the roads) who were invited to the great supper represent the Gentiles. God had promised in His Word that He would send His Savior, the Messiah, into the world for the Jews first and then for all the Gentiles. A Gentile is anyone who is not Jewish.

Have you accepted the invitation of Jesus? If you are His follower, are you enjoying a close relationship with Him? Are you spending time in God's Word and in prayer daily? Are you leading others to Christ? Consider how you might draw closer to Christ starting today.

*Lord, how sad that so many reject Your invitation!
Thank You that I have You in my heart. Help me
grow closer to You day by day. Amen.*

DON'T CAUSE OTHERS TO STUMBLE

Jesus said to His followers, "For sure, things will come that will make people sin. But it is bad for the person who makes someone else sin. It would be better for him to have a large rock put around his neck and be thrown into the sea, than that he should cause one of these little ones to sin."

LUKE 17:1–2

Here Jesus warns against causing a new Christian, a "baby in the faith," to lose her faith. He says that if someone becomes a stumbling block to such a Christian, it would be better for him to have a large rock tied around his neck and be thrown into the sea. Those are harsh words! This is a warning we all should heed.

Be sure your actions are not confusing to new believers. For example, if others know you say you're a Christ follower and you're active in your church, live in a way that honors Christ. Certainly, no one is perfect! But if you proclaim to be a believer yet live a lifestyle that opposes Christ, you may cause less mature Christians to stumble. They might ask, "Why should I live in a godly manner if so-and-so is taking part in these sinful activities?"

Jesus, help me never to be a stumbling block
to anyone. Instead, help me set a good
example of godly living for others. Amen.

FORGIVE OTHERS

*"What if he sins against you seven times in one day?
If he comes to you and says he is sorry and
turns from his sin, forgive him."*

LUKE 17:4

Have you ever played the "What If" game? Sometimes kids will create a scenario and ask a parent what they would do "if. . ." For example, What if I flooded the bathroom? What if I got a real tattoo? What if I jumped off the roof? What if. . . ? The list goes on and on. The imagination runs wild. The kids always want answers to their "what if" questions.

What if someone sins against you seven times in one day? Jesus knows this is a question His followers wish to have answered. So He answers it plain and simple. We are to forgive. There is no limit to forgiveness. Certainly, we may have to draw boundaries in order to stay safe from someone who repeatedly hurts us. Christ is not saying here to just allow repeated hurt again and again.

As you consider all that Jesus has forgiven you for, are you led to grow in your forgiveness of others? Be quick to forgive. It pleases the Lord.

Lord, help me forgive others freely and quickly—
again and again and again, just as You forgive me. Amen.

THE ONE WHO SAID THANK YOU

Jesus asked, "Were there not ten men who were healed? Where are the other nine? Is this stranger from another country the only one who turned back to give thanks to God?" Then Jesus said to him, "Get up and go on your way. Your trust in God has healed you."

Jesus healed ten men. They were lepers, suffering a horrible disease of sores from head to toe. They were outcasts of society because of it. They were miserable, and then. . .they were healed. Their sickness fled. The disease disappeared. Their bodies were clear of the awful sores that had been there just a moment before. They were miraculously set free from the leprosy that had bound them.

There were ten.

But only one wanted more of Jesus. Only one fell at His feet. Only one thanked Him. Just one. And that one was given more than physical healing that day. His faith and devotion and his mere thankfulness gave him spiritual healing.

It didn't matter that he was a Samaritan (Jews did not associate with Samaritans). Jesus touched him, cleansed him, and made him new. And when the man fell at Jesus' feet, Jesus told him to get up. He set him free from sores and from sin. He gave him eternal life.

Lord, may I always remember to thank You.
Help me to be grateful like the one man who fell at
Your feet when You took away his leprosy. Amen.

THE PROUD RELIGIOUS LAW-KEEPERS AND THE TAX COLLECTOR

"I tell you, this man went back to his house forgiven, and not the other man. For whoever makes himself look more important than he is will find out how little he is worth. Whoever does not try to honor himself will be made important."

LUKE 18:14

Jesus told a parable of two men. They were different in every way. One was a rule keeper, a religious man, who followed the law and was proud to say he did. The other was a tax collector. Tax collectors were not popular with the people in Bible days. They profited from the people's tax money and sometimes collected more than they should.

The religious man in the picture-story prayed a showy prayer, saying how glad he was that he wasn't like those who sin. He was thankful he was not like the tax collector. In his prayer, he told of his own wonderful acts, such as how he fasted and how he gave to the Lord's work.

Meanwhile, the tax collector beat his own chest. He cried out to God that he was a sinner and begged the Lord to have pity on him.

Which man was forgiven? The tax collector, Jesus said, went home forgiven that day.

Don't seek to honor yourself. Seek to honor God.

Father in heaven, I recognize that I am not worthy of forgiveness or blessing and that these things come to me only by Your great grace. Amen.

PRAY FIRST

*Jesus said to them, "There is much grain ready
to gather. But the workmen are few. Pray then to
the Lord Who is the Owner of the grain-fields that
He will send workmen to gather His grain."*

LUKE 10:2

Going out to share the gospel with others is wonderful. But it requires preparation. In the book of Luke, we read about a mission of seventy disciples whom Jesus was about to send out. The first instruction Jesus gave this group of evangelists was to pray. They were told to pray for more workers to gather the grain.

What does this mean? Well, the fact that there was "much grain ready to gather" means there was a lot of work to do to spread the gospel to everyone. Many would come to Jesus, but they needed to be located, told about Jesus, and "harvested."

Who is the owner of the grain-fields? You guessed it—God.

These men were to ask God to send more help to spread the gospel. They were also praying for full participation of all the workers who were already working.

*Lord, may I always pray before I start
any mission to lead others to Christ. Amen.*

THE GOAL OF THE MISSION

"Take no money. Do not take a bag or shoes.
Speak to no one along the way."

LUKE 10:4

When Jesus instructed the seventy He sent out to share the gospel, He told them to travel lightly. They were not to take money, bags, or even shoes. He wanted them to depend on God. God would provide all they needed through the kindness and generosity of believers. These gifts would sustain them—keep them alive and going.

When they were told not to speak along the way, Jesus didn't mean that the disciples should be unfriendly. He wasn't asking them to be rude or ugly. But in that day, a greeting could be very long. An ancient Middle Eastern greeting could literally take days! Jesus wanted these men to keep their goal always in mind. They had a mission to bring in a great harvest of new believers. They were to pursue this quest and not waste time on things that were less important.

We can apply this idea to our own missions today. Keep the goal in mind. If someone shows no interest in your message of the good news, it's time to move on. Share it with someone who is ready and willing to hear about Jesus.

Lord, may I be focused on sharing the gospel
so that others may come to know You. Amen.

EXCITEMENT FOR THE MISSION

"Even so, you should not be happy because the demons obey you but be happy because your names are written in heaven."

LUKE 10:20

The seventy who were sent out were given great power that could come only from Jesus. He gave them the power to cast out demons, among other abilities. When they returned after their mission, they reported their success to Jesus, excited that they had been allowed to witness such great victories over evil.

While the casting out of demons was definitely a wonderful benefit of the evangelistic journey these men had been on, Jesus reminded them that what was most important was that God would remember their diligent service. Not only had they have been saved, but their names were recorded in heaven as faithful followers of the Lord.

It's exciting when someone we know is saved. It's thrilling to experience the victories and joys that occur while on a mission of serving God. Even greater is our reward in heaven!

Lord, I am thankful for my salvation. Please help me be a faithful servant so that my name might be recorded in Your book. Amen.

TEACHER?

A man stood up who knew the Law and tried
to trap Jesus. He said, "Teacher, what must I do
to have life that lasts forever?" Jesus said to him,
"What is written in the Law? What does the Law say?"

LUKE 10:25–26

This scripture passage includes several small details that we might miss if we don't study the context, the background of the story. We read in Luke 10:25 that a man who knew the law tested Jesus. This would have been a man who was an expert in the law given by Moses.

When the man calls Jesus "Teacher," the title sounds respectful. It sounds like a title of honor and authority. The truth is that this term was lower than *Prophet* or *Messiah* or. . .*God*. The man saw Jesus as lower than these. He referred to Him as Teacher.

He wanted Jesus' opinion of how one receives eternal life. Instead of just giving the man the answer, Jesus responded by referring to the Old Testament law, which both of them would agree was true and important. Jesus was never trapped, never tricked, and never backed into a corner. He would often answer in such a way that caused the one asking to think deeper or to come to the conclusion himself.

Lord, You are more than a teacher or prophet.
You are the Messiah, my Savior. You are God, the
Father, the Son, and the Holy Spirit. Amen.

KEEPING THE LAW

*Jesus said to him, "You have said the right thing. Do this
and you will have life." The man tried to make himself
look good. He asked Jesus, "Who is my neighbor?"*

LUKE 10:28–29

The man who questioned Jesus in Luke 10 knew the answer. He stated clearly to Jesus that in order to receive eternal life, "you must love the Lord your God with all your heart. You must love Him with all your soul. You must love Him with all your strength. You must love Him with all your mind. You must love your neighbor as you love yourself" (verse 27).

Instead of admitting there was no possible way to fully keep this law because no one is perfect, the man tried to make himself look good. He asked Jesus who his neighbor was. Certainly the Samaritans and foreigners would not be included! Or would they?

This man realized the only way he could keep that law was to limit what it demanded of him. He loved people like him. Maybe that would be enough!

Jesus did not answer the man's question directly but told of the good Samaritan. The question is clearly answered in that story. Anyone in need is considered to be our "neighbor," regardless of their race or social status.

Lord, how sad that some are not willing to receive the free gift of eternal life. Instead, they try to work for it. Thank You for my salvation and that I have been given eternal life with You. Amen.

BE A GOOD NEIGHBOR

*"A religious leader was walking down that road and saw
the man. But he went by on the other side. In the same way,
a man from the family group of Levi was walking down that
road. When he saw the man who was hurt, he came near
to him but kept on going on the other side of the road. Then
a man from the country of Samaria came by. He went up
to the man. As he saw him, he had loving-pity on him."*

LUKE 10:31-33

A man was lying on the side of the road. He had been beaten and left
to die. Two people passed him by, ignoring his great need. A third
person stopped and took care of him.

Who was the good neighbor? Obviously it was the Samaritan.

Who can you be a neighbor to? Who can you go out of your way
to help this week? Maybe you could stop by a nursing home and
brighten some residents' day just by listening to them or reading a
book or playing a game with them. Do you have a younger sibling
who would love for you to include her when you play with friends?
Maybe you've noticed someone who always sits alone in the school
cafeteria or on the bus. Could you invite him to join your group?

*Jesus, help me see past race, religion, and money.
Help me be a good neighbor to anyone in need. Amen.*

DON'T WORRY ABOUT MATERIAL THINGS

Jesus said to His followers, "Because of this, I say to you, do not worry about your life, what you are going to eat. Do not worry about your body, what you are going to wear. Life is worth more than food. The body is worth more than clothes."

LUKE 12:22–23

Jesus was talking with His disciples. He made sure they knew they shouldn't worry about material possessions. He wanted them to see that there is more to life than food and clothing. These are needs of the present life here on earth. Food and clothing are not going to last forever. They meet temporary needs and one day will be of no use. They are just covering (clothing) and fuel (food). The disciples were to treat them as secondary needs, not the most important thing. And we should follow this advice as well.

We're also warned not to be greedy with our material possessions (Luke 12:15). They are just things and one day will be burned up and forgotten. Instead, we should focus on spiritual matters.

Lord, help me keep things in perspective. When I begin to desire things or worry about them, remind me that really they are just "extras." One day they will mean nothing at all. What matters is my walk with You! Amen.

IF GOD CARES FOR THE BIRDS. . .

"Look at the birds. They do not plant seeds. They do not gather grain. They have no grain buildings for keeping grain. Yet God feeds them. Are you not worth more than the birds?"

LUKE 12:24

In the King James Version of the Bible, this verse says, "Consider the ravens: for they neither sow nor reap; which neither have storehouse nor barn; and God feedeth them: how much more are ye better than the fowls?"

It is interesting that Jesus chose to use the raven as an example of God providing for His creatures. Ravens, in Jesus' day, were considered to be unclean (Leviticus 11:15). They are known for not feeding their young, but God takes care of that. He sees to it that even the young ravens eat. If God takes care of the birds (even the ravens!), how much more will He take care of humans!

People are God's masterpiece. He created us last as a finishing touch to His creation! We are made in His image. We never need to worry that God has forgotten us. He will always provide what we need. People are very important to God.

Lord, thank You for taking care of me and providing for my needs. Calm my fears about the future. I know that You are in control of my life and You are my provider. Amen.

BE HUMBLE

"Whoever makes himself look more important than
he is will find out how little he is worth. Whoever does
not try to honor himself will be made important."

LUKE 14:11

This parable of the wedding supper is about how people should relate to God. Humility is all-important. We must recognize that God is the host and we are merely invited to the banquet (invited into the kingdom).

When Jesus spoke these words, He was originally using them to correct the Pharisees' pride. It was clear that the Pharisees wanted themselves to be important, rather than follow the one who is worthy of all praise, honor, and glory. Christ called them to humble themselves and follow Him as disciples.

A person's role or position in the kingdom of God is determined not by self but by God. Lowering your opinion of yourself in the here and now on earth will result in being lifted up by God in the future, in heaven.

Lord, help me be humble. Help me remember
that I serve You, the holy God, and that I am
a sinner saved only by Your grace. Amen.

CARRY YOUR CROSS

Then Jesus said to them all, "If anyone wants to follow Me,
he must give up himself and his own desires. He must
take up his cross everyday and follow Me."

LUKE 9:23

If you want to follow Jesus, you need to be "all in." During Christ's ministry on earth, many people gathered near to Him who did not wish to truly follow Him. They wanted the benefits of healing and miracles. They were curious, but they were not interested in laying down their desires in order to follow the Savior.

When a criminal was walking to his crucifixion in Jesus' day, he often carried part of his cross himself. So when we are called to take up our cross every day and follow Jesus, it means we are to accept the hardships of living the Christian life. There will be things we cannot have or do because we follow Jesus. There will be a burden, a weight, that we must carry. Are you willing to follow Jesus in this way?

To truly take up your cross and follow Him, you must realize that it could even cost your life. But Jesus willingly gave His life for you. Would you give yours for Him if you were called to do so?

Jesus, may I take up my cross and follow
hard after You all the days of my life. Amen.

WHAT IS YOUR CROSS?

*"If he does not carry his cross and follow
Me, he cannot be My follower."*

LUKE 14:27

Here we read again about taking up our cross to follow Christ. What is your cross? What is it that you need to give up or lay down so that you can fully follow Jesus?

For you right now, it might mean that you lay down being popular at school or in the neighborhood or even in a church group. That's tough. It feels good to be well liked and admired. Maybe being an all-in Christian is not "cool" in those groups. Be one anyway.

Carrying your cross might be staying true to Jesus even though it costs you a friend's or family member's approval. You want that person to be happy with you, maybe even proud of you. But Jesus asks you to want Him more than anything—even another's approval. When it hurts, follow anyway.

Maybe you've been asked to join an elite sports team. But all the games are on Sundays and you would have to miss church. Consider that this may be something you need to lay down in order to experience true blessing.

Whatever desire you must give up, whatever loss you must suffer—Jesus is worth it. Pray now and ask God to reveal to you what "carrying your cross" means to you personally in your life right now.

Lord, show me my cross and help me to be
willing to carry it—every day. Amen.

DO NOT PUT THINGS ABOVE JESUS

*"In the same way, whoever does not give up
all that he has, cannot be My follower."*

LUKE 14:33

Jesus wasn't telling the people they had to go and sell everything they owned in order to follow Him, becoming completely broke. And as a Christian today, you are not called to do that either.

What Jesus meant here is that we shouldn't place great value on material things. We should wisely manage the material possessions we have and be willing and ready to give up any of them as we are called to. They shouldn't get in the way of bringing glory to God or fulfilling our calling to tell others about Jesus. We should live simply. We should think and ask, Is anything blocking me from being faithful to the Lord? If so, root it out. Give it away.

As believers in Christ, we need to be willing to give up *things* in order to have more of Him. What are you willing to lay down? What might you need to get rid of because it distracts or tempts you? What *things* are taking more of your time, money, or energy than Jesus? Pray about this and be ready to hear His answer and act on it.

Lord, show me if there are things getting in
the way of my relationship with You. Amen.

DON'T LOSE YOUR SALTINESS

"Salt is good. But if salt has lost its taste, how can it be made to taste like salt again? It is no good for the field or the waste place. Men throw it away. You have ears, then listen!"

LUKE 14:34–35

Jesus compares His disciples, those who followed Him, to salt. If you begin following Jesus but don't continue to follow Him as a priority in your life, you "lose your saltiness." Salt that is not salty is useless. And a Christian who no longer follows Jesus is useless.

If you fall away from following Christ, there is a danger, not of losing your salvation, but of losing some of your reward in the future. Perhaps you will miss out on opportunities He had planned for you for greater service in this life or in eternity.

Stay true to Jesus. This is a serious warning. Don't lose your saltiness.

The words to an old song ring true today: "I have decided to follow Jesus, no turning back, no turning back."

Lord, I have chosen to follow You. Please help me focus on You and You alone. Help me not to get distracted or fall away because I experience loss or disappointment. Keep my eyes fixed on You so that I might be useful to Your kingdom now and in eternity. Amen.

SPIRITUALLY BLIND

Some of the proud religious law-keepers who were with Him
heard this. They said to Him, "Are we blind also?" Jesus said
to them, "If you were blind, you would not be guilty of sin.
But because you say, 'We see,' you still are guilty of your sin."

JOHN 9:40–41

Even though the religious leaders of Jesus' day were very knowledge-able, they were far from wise. Sure, they knew a lot about the Old Testament law, but they rejected Jesus when it was very clear that He was, in fact, the Son of God.

They thought Jesus might be calling them "spiritually blind," and they couldn't believe their ears! They thought they were the wisest and most enlightened men of all! In fact, Jesus' words revealed that it was as if they were walking around in total darkness, refusing to accept spiritual truth.

This still happens today. Sometimes those who need Jesus the most don't recognize their need. They are too busy thinking highly of themselves. Even the most educated or intelligent human being is spiritually blind if they refuse to accept the gift of salvation offered only through Christ.

Jesus, thank You for giving me eyes to see the truth.
Please continue to reveal to me more and more of Yourself
through Your Word as I read and study. Amen.

JESUS IS LORD

Jesus said to [the man healed of blindness], "You have seen Him. He is talking with you." He said, "I do put my trust in You, Lord." Then he bowed down before Jesus and worshiped Him.

JOHN 9:37–38

Jesus healed a man who was blind from birth. Earlier, Christ had healed those who had been blinded due to accidents, but this is the first time we read of Him healing someone who was born without sight. When Jesus did this miracle, He showed that He was able to heal those in the very worst and most desperate situations. He was not limited in His power.

After Jesus healed the man, He revealed Himself as the Son of God to the man. The man had faith in Jesus to begin with, which is why he was healed. But he had not fully understood who Jesus was.

As we move through the verses in John 9 that tell this story, we read that he first called Jesus "a Man called Jesus" (verse 11), then "One Who speaks for God" (verse 17), and finally he labeled Him clearly with the word "Lord" (verse 38).

The Pharisees continued to reject Jesus, but this one who had been given sight knew and believed that Jesus was the Son of God. He fell flat on his face before Christ and worshipped Him.

Lord, I am so thankful that You brought me out of darkness and into the light when You saved me. Please continue to teach me more about who You are. Amen.

JESUS' PERFECT TIMING

When the wine was all gone, the mother of Jesus said to Him,
"They have no more wine." Jesus said to her, "Woman, what
is that to you and to Me. It is not time for Me to work yet."

JOHN 2:3–4

Have you ever been to a wedding? It's like a big party! After the bride and groom are married, everyone celebrates. In Jesus' day, these celebrations were very special.

One day Jesus and His disciples were invited to a wedding. The host ran out of wine, and Mary, the mother of Jesus, wanted Him to do something. Some think she wanted Him to go and buy wine, but most scholars agree Mary wanted Jesus to do something miraculous to solve the problem. But Jesus clearly told her it wasn't the right time yet.

He didn't say He wouldn't help or that wine wouldn't be provided. But He did let Mary know that He wouldn't be rushed.

Have you ever wanted Jesus to do something on your timetable? Did He seem to be running late? Jesus is never late. He is always right on time. His timing may not match ours, and we may wonder why He waits to answer some of our requests, but like Mary, we must trust that Jesus knows what He is doing.

Lord, please give me faith and help me
to trust Your perfect timing. Amen.

WATER TO WINE

*Jesus said to the helpers, "Fill the jars with water." They filled
them to the top. Then He said, "Take some out and give it to
the head man who is caring for the people." They took some to
him. The head man tasted the water that had become wine.
He did not know where it came from but the helpers who took
it to him knew. He called the man who had just been married.
The head man said to him, "Everyone puts out his best wine
first. After people have had much to drink, he puts out the wine
that is not so good. You have kept the good wine until now!"*

JOHN 2:7–10

Have you ever been to a party where the drinks ran out early? Maybe
you went back for more lemonade or another root beer float only to
be told that there was nothing left to drink but water.

In Bible times, wine was very important at a wedding celebration. The wine was served by the host as a way to show how much
he appreciated the guests. Running out of wine was a bad thing!
People expected to have wine at a wedding, and running out of it
made the host look bad.

At just the right time, Jesus turned water into wine. When this miracle
took place, the glory of Jesus was revealed and the disciples trusted in
Jesus. They knew He was the Son of God.

Jesus, thank You for Your miracles
that show You are God. Amen.

A RIDDLE

Jesus answered them, "Destroy this house of God and in three days I will build it again." Then the Jews said, "It took forty-six years to build this house of God. Will You build it up in three days?" Jesus was speaking of His body as the house of God.

JOHN 2:19–21

The Jews were testing Jesus. They weren't truly interested in following Him and trusting in Him as their Savior. Jesus knew that. So when they came to Him asking for a miracle, He responded with a sort of riddle.

He told them that if they were to destroy the temple, He would rebuild it in only three days. This indeed would have proved that He had supernatural powers and was from God! But they were not willing to destroy the temple.

Jesus was not speaking about the actual temple, although He had come to replace the old temple with a new one and a new way of worship. He was talking about His own body, which would rise from the dead after three days in the grave. One day, after Jesus' resurrection, these words would make sense and Jesus' followers would understand them.

Jesus answered in a riddle on purpose. He did this often in order to hide truth from unbelievers but show it to believers.

Lord, increase my belief and trust in You, I pray. Amen.

OBEYING JESUS

Then Jesus said to them, "Children, do you have any fish?"
They said, "No." He said to them, "Put your net over the right side
of the boat. Then you will catch some fish." They put out the net.
They were not able to pull it in because it was so full of fish.

JOHN 21:5–6

The disciples didn't know it was Jesus who greeted them and asked if they had caught any fish. We don't know exactly why. Perhaps it was due to the twilight. Maybe Jesus was too great a distance from them to be identified. Maybe His appearance was different after being raised from the dead. We don't know, but what we do know is that they didn't know it was Jesus.

Yet when this unidentified person told them to try putting their net on the other side of the boat, they followed His instructions. They did what He said, and a miracle occurred. They had so many fish in the net that they couldn't even pull it in.

Jesus wants His followers to obey Him. There is great reward for those who obey the Word of the Lord. Jesus is able to do more than we could even imagine.

Lord, help me trust and obey your Word in every area of my life. I know there is great reward in doing so. Amen.

COME AND EAT

Jesus said to them, "Come and eat." Not one of the followers would ask, "Who are You?" They knew it was the Lord. Jesus came and took bread and fish and gave it to them.

JOHN 21:12–13

Jesus was the host of this breakfast on the shore. He had, after all, provided the fish. This was His third appearance to the disciples, and although, for whatever reason, they were not able to tell by His appearance that He was Jesus, they knew deep down He was their Lord.

In that day in the ancient Middle East, if someone provided a meal for you, it was a promise to protect and defend you from that day forward. Jesus might have been using this breakfast of fish and bread to say to His disciples that He was committed to them. The guests at such a meal were, when they accepted the invitation, also committing themselves to the host. Just as Jesus was promising to be loyal to them, the disciples were recommitting themselves to the Lord as well.

> Lord, may I always recognize You in my life.
> May I see Your hand at work and be thankful
> for the way You provide for my needs. Amen.

RESISTING TEMPTATION TO SIN

But Jesus said, "It is written, 'Man is not to live on bread only. Man is to live by every word that God speaks.'"

MATTHEW 4:4

The devil tempted Jesus by telling Him to turn stones into bread. Jesus had been in the wilderness without food for forty days and nights. Can you imagine how hungry He was? Yet He didn't fall to Satan's temptation.

Jesus stood up to Satan, not through supernatural powers but through the Word of God and the Holy Spirit. We also have both of those to help us fight back against the evil one. Jesus did this so that He would be a perfect example for us of how we can stand up to Satan.

Satan tempted Jesus when He was vulnerable. He didn't come to Jesus and try to get Him to turn rocks into food after Jesus had eaten a delicious meal. He came to Him when He was weak, after a long period of time without food.

Satan will try to tempt us when we are at our weakest moments also. Remember to use the Bible to help you resist temptation to sin, and call upon the Holy Spirit for help as well.

Jesus, I ask that You would give me strength to resist temptation. Amen.

LOYALTY TO GOD

*He said to Jesus, "I will give You all these nations if You will
get down at my feet and worship me." Jesus said to the
devil, "Get away, Satan. It is written, 'You must worship the
Lord your God. You must obey Him only.'" Then the devil
went away from Jesus. Angels came and cared for Him.*

MATTHEW 4:9–11

Satan had the power to give Jesus what he offered him here. Jesus
could have taken the bait. He would have been a slave to Satan but
also a world ruler. Instead Jesus told him to "get away." He told Satan
that the Lord must be worshipped and the Lord only must be obeyed.

At that very moment when Christ showed utter loyalty to God,
Satan went away from Jesus. He did as Jesus commanded. He tempo-
rarily left. God then instantly rewarded Jesus. He sent angels to take
care of Jesus. God helped Jesus and would give Him more chances for
service in the future. This is how God normally operates.

If you are faithful to God and if you resist temptation and honor
Him, He will bless you. You will receive rewards in either this life or
the next, in heaven. God sees you when you rely on His Word and
His Spirit to defeat Satan. Stand firm against the temptations of
the evil one.

*God, I ask You to strengthen me that I might stand
up against Satan's attacks on my life. I know there
is great reward in remaining loyal to You. Amen.*

HEAVEN AND HELL

*"And more than all this, there is a big deep place
between us. No one from here can go there even
if he wanted to go. No one can come from there."*

LUKE 16:26

Each one of us will live eternally. Our souls will exist after this life. When we take our final breath on this earth, this life comes to an end and the next life begins. If you are a believer in Jesus Christ, you know that your eternity is secure and you will live with Jesus forever. Heaven will be your eternal home.

Hell is as real as heaven. It is a real place, and unbelievers will live out their eternity there. Choices made in this life have consequences. Those who choose to reject Jesus are giving up the opportunity to have eternal life with Him in glory. They are trading paradise for a lake of fire.

Jesus made it very clear that heaven and hell are real. What a great promise we have as Christians that we know where we are headed! Pray for unbelievers. Share the gospel with them. Take every chance you have to lead the lost to Christ.

*Lord Jesus, lead me to those who are lost and give me
boldness to share the good news with them. Amen.*

166

WHAT REALLY MATTERS IN LIFE

"The poor man who asked for food died. He was taken by the angels into the arms of Abraham. The rich man died also and was buried."

LUKE 16:22

Outward appearance, wealth, and reputation are only for this life. In the next life, things will be very different. Jesus told a parable, or picture-story, in order to teach about the "tables turning."

He told about a rich man and a poor man. The rich man went to hell, and the poor man received a blessed eternity in heaven. He was met and welcomed by heroes of the faith, such as Abraham!

It is not important how much stuff you have or how big your home is. It's not important if you go to an elite, expensive school or a public one. It may seem to matter in this life, but in the end, it matters not. Where you spend eternity depends on one thing. It depends on what you do with Jesus Christ. When you hear the good news, do you accept it or reject it? Is Jesus just another man, a prophet, or a good teacher? Or do you believe in your heart that He is the way, the truth, and the life and that no one comes to the Father except through Him?

The answers to these questions make a big difference. Make sure you get this right.

Jesus, I believe You are the Son of God and that You died for my sins. Forgive me, set me free, and give me assurance of my eternity with You, I ask. Amen.

ONLY ONE BOSS

"No servant can have two bosses. He will hate the one and love the other. Or, he will be faithful to one and not faithful to the other. You cannot be faithful to God and to riches at the same time."

LUKE 16:13

Have you ever tried to please two groups of people and found it impossible? Maybe your friends are pressuring you to do one thing on the weekend, but your parents want you to do something different. You try to figure out a way to do both things to please both your friends and your parents. But in the end, it is often impossible to do so. You have to choose. Who wins out? Who is more important to you?

Jesus said that it is impossible to be loyal to both money and God. One will win out. One will matter more to you. Which is more precious to you? Which is your true master?

Before you answer, consider this. How do you spend most of your time? What do you desire most in life? Are your thoughts filled with material things or spiritual matters? Are you as hungry for the Word of God as you are for that item at the top of your Christmas list?

Things will pass away. They will burn up one day. Money will mean nothing when you take your last breath in this life. Choose your master well. You cannot serve both material wealth and God.

Lord, I want to be known as someone who chooses You every time. Deepen my loyalty, I pray. May I never make anyone or anything more important than You. Amen.

MUSTARD SEED FAITH

*The Lord said, "If your faith was as a mustard seed,
you could say to this tree, 'Be pulled out of the ground
and planted in the sea,' and it would obey you."*

LUKE 17:6

When the disciples asked for more faith, Jesus told them they didn't need more. They simply needed to use the faith they already had. He used the picture-story of a mustard seed. A mustard seed is very tiny, and Jesus surprised the disciples by telling them how much power even "mustard seed faith" has.

He told them that if they had even a tiny amount of faith the size of a mustard seed, they could command a mulberry tree to be uprooted and planted in the sea. That would be miraculous!

In other words, even a very small amount of faith in Christ is enough to do extremely big things!

If you have a little bit of faith, use it. Step out in faith, and you will do great things for the kingdom of God. Don't worry if you see another person who seems to have a much greater amount of faith. Be thankful that you have some faith—even "mustard seed faith"—and use it to make a big difference in the world for Jesus.

Lord, thank You for the faith I have. May I act on it boldly
so that much good is done for Your kingdom. Amen.

THE BELIEVER'S ATTITUDE

"It is the same with you also. When you do everything you have been told to do, you must say, 'We are not any special servants. We have done only what we should have done.'"

LUKE 17:10

Have you ever made the mistake of asking your parent what you will get if you do a task, such as cleaning your room? You may have received this answer: "Get? You will get a warm feeling in your heart because you know you did the right thing!" It is never wise to expect a reward—as if when you are doing the right thing, you deserve something extra. You do the right thing because you are motivated in your heart to do the right thing.

Jesus warned His disciples, who were His closest followers, against such an attitude. The Pharisees of that day believed that if they did good things, God owed them a reward. But Jesus told the disciples, for example, that warning another disciple who sinned or forgiving those who repented of sin was their responsibility. It was their duty. Kind of like how cleaning your room is your duty. They weren't to feel that God owed them something afterward.

God rewards believers for faithful service—out of His mercy and grace, not out of a debt owed to any human being. Jesus wants His followers to watch their attitudes when serving. God expects our service; it's not something extra that God needs to "tip" you for doing.

Lord, may I do good for the sake of
doing good and nothing more. Amen.

CHILDREN ARE IMPORTANT

Jesus called the followers to Him and said, "Let the little children come to Me. Do not try to stop them. The holy nation of God is made up of ones like these. For sure, I tell you, whoever does not receive the holy nation of God as a child will not go into the holy nation."

LUKE 18:16–17

Have you ever felt as if you were not important just because you're a kid? Maybe you were in a room full of adults, and you almost felt invisible. Everyone was chattering around you and eating and drinking. You were just there, and no one seemed to know you even existed!

Children are special to Jesus. We know this to be true because when the parents were trying to take their children to Jesus, the disciples scolded them. They tried to keep the children back from the busy Savior, but Jesus said to let the little children come to Him. He told His disciples not to try to stop them. He took time for them. He held them. He blessed them.

Jesus reminded people that they must have the faith of a child in order to receive eternal life. Just the simple, trusting faith of a child.

Lord, thank You for valuing me even though I am young. I feel so special when I read in the Bible that You welcomed children and that they were important to You. Amen.

CAN A RICH PERSON GO TO HEAVEN?

When Jesus saw that [the leader] was very sad, He said,
"It is hard for those with riches to go into the holy nation of
God! It is easier for a camel to go through the eye of a needle
than for a rich man to go into the holy nation of God."

LUKE 18:24–25

Why do you think Jesus said it was difficult for a rich person to get into heaven? Think about it. The rich may be distracted by worldly possessions and money. Also, they may believe they are better than or superior to the poor and that they are not in need of salvation. After all, if you have more in this world, you often have more fame or power. The rich may not plan for the future because they think they are secure in their treasures.

All that will matter in the end is what we have done with Jesus in this life. Can the rich accept Christ and live a Christian life? Certainly! Many wealthy people know Jesus as their Savior. You find them using their money, homes, vehicles, and other resources for God's glory.

When Jesus told one wealthy man in the Bible that he needed to give up his possessions in order to follow Christ, the man went away sad. He had the opportunity to receive Jesus and eternal life, but he gave it up for the things of this world. How many people do the same today!

Lord, thank You that I know You and that I know
I will spend eternity in heaven with You. Amen.

JESUS KNEW HE WAS GOING TO DIE

"He will be given over to the people who are not Jews. He will be made fun of. He will be hurt. He will be spit on. They will beat Him and kill Him. After three days He will be raised again."

LUKE 18:32–33

Jesus died for us willingly. He knew His death was coming. He told about it, but the people could not understand until after it had taken place.

Can you imagine knowing that your death was near? Jesus knew, yet He did nothing to try to flee. He continued His ministry on earth right up to the very last. He didn't fight the soldiers who came to take Him away. In fact, He stopped His disciples from defending Him. He went with the soldiers out of His own will.

Certainly, Jesus asked God if there was another way as He prayed in the garden. His humanity knew that death would be painful. He would have preferred to avoid the torture of death upon a cross. But when there was no other way, He accepted God's will, went to the cross, and died a terrible death for you and me.

Jesus gave His life for you. Now live yours for Him in return!

Lord Jesus, thank You for dying once for all upon the cross. You sacrificed Your very life for me. Help me now to live my life for You. Amen.

EVEN A TAX COLLECTOR

Zaccheus stood up and said to the Lord, "Lord, see! Half of what I own I will give to poor people. And if I have taken money from anyone in a wrong way, I will pay him back four times as much." Jesus said to him, "Today, a person has been saved in this house. This man is a Jew also. For the Son of Man came to look for and to save from the punishment of sin those who are lost."

LUKE 19:8–10

You know the story of the "wee little man" named Zaccheus. Sure, a short man climbed a tree to see Jesus. But what is really important is that Jesus saw Zaccheus. Jesus saw the faith that this tax collector had. Why would Zaccheus make such a great effort to see Jesus if he was not interested in discovering the Savior?

At the very end of the children's song about Zaccheus, we hear these words: "Zaccheus, you come down from there, for I'm going to your house today! For I'm going to your house today!" Jesus said these words.

And do you know what happened that day? Zaccheus turned from sin and accepted the Savior. He left a life of stealing from people and not only returned their money but also gave them even more than he had taken in the first place!

Tax collectors were not respected in Jesus' day. The story of Zaccheus shows that Jesus can save anyone who repents of sin and turns his life toward the Lord.

Jesus, thank You for saving sinners, including me! Amen.

GIVE SACRIFICIALLY

He saw a poor woman whose husband had died. She put in two very small pieces of money. He said, "I tell you the truth, this poor woman has put in more than all of them. For they have put in a little of the money they had no need for. She is very poor and has put in all she had. She has put in what she needed for her own living."

LUKE 21:2–4

✦ ✦ ✦

Have you ever received a gift from a younger child? Maybe a picture she drew or a rock she found on the playground? Even though the gift is small, it feels important since you know the child is giving all she has. You know the gift comes from the child's heart.

The same was true of a woman whose husband had died. In Jesus' day, a widow was in a scary position because women depended on men to provide for them. This woman was poor. Instead of keeping what she had, she gave all she had to the Lord. She didn't even save enough to meet her own needs.

Jesus said this small gift was worth far more than the little amount given by those who had a lot of money. They didn't give up anything they needed. Be sure that when you give, you give sacrificially. Maybe you will need to go without something in order to give to the Lord.

Lord, help me give to You in the way the widow did.
May my gifts be pleasing to You. Amen.

THE FIRST LORD'S SUPPER

[Jesus] said to them, "I have wanted very much to eat this special supper with you to remember how the Jews left Egypt. I have wanted to eat this with you before I suffer. I say to you, I will not eat this special supper again until its true meaning is completed in the holy nation of God."

LUKE 22:15–16

Do you have an object that reminds you of someone special? Maybe you wear a necklace that a parent or grandparent gave to you. Perhaps your dad or grandpa passed down a special football or basketball that is now yours. Those items mean a lot to us even if they are not of great value to others. They have sentimental value. You may even have something that used to belong to a family member or friend who has passed away. Such items bring that person to our memory.

Have you ever seen or taken part in the Lord's Supper at your church? Do you know the history and meaning of it? It's not something that the modern church made up to remember Jesus. It was actually created by Jesus, and He told His followers to use it to remember Him. When Jesus broke bread and shared wine with His disciples on the night before His death, He shared with them the special meaning of the bread and wine. He told them to partake of the bread and wine as a way to remember Him always.

Lord, may I always remember Your life, death, and resurrection. May I take part in the Lord's Supper with other believers as a special remembrance time. Amen.

THE BODY OF JESUS

*Then Jesus took bread and gave thanks and broke it
in pieces. He gave it to them, saying, "This is My body
which is given for you. Do this to remember Me."*

LUKE 22:19

The body of Christ was broken for you. That is powerful. When we take communion, or the Lord's Supper, we eat a small piece of bread or a cracker to represent Jesus' body.

While it is not really the body of Jesus, it brings to mind that Jesus' body was cruelly broken on the cross for us. He bled and died a death that involved a lot of pain and torture. He took our sins upon Himself. While He was a sinless man, He bore the sins of the whole world that day. What a burden He took on His shoulders to the cross—the weight of the world.

When you eat the cracker or the bread during communion (the Lord's Supper), remember Christ's body that was given for you.

Lord Jesus, thank You for dying on the cross for my sins.
As I take the bread, I remember Your death and that
You allowed Your body to be broken for me. Amen.

177

THE BLOOD OF JESUS

*In the same way, after they had finished the bread,
He took the cup. He said, "This cup is My blood of the
New Way of Worship which is given for you."*

LUKE 22:20

Have you ever held your hand against your heart or touched the inside of your wrist with two fingers? What do you feel when you do this? You feel a pulse, don't you? That is blood pumping through your body, giving you life.

In the Old Testament, blood had to be shed in order for sins to be forgiven. The people followed the law in sacrificing certain types of animals for particular sins. These rituals had to be followed in order for the sinner to receive God's forgiveness.

Jesus Christ was the perfect lamb. His death was the sacrifice for us. He died in our place. His blood paid the price for our wrongdoing.

When you take the cup of wine or juice during the Lord's Supper (communion), remember that Jesus' blood was poured out for you. Because He bled and died, you have abundant life and you are promised eternal life with Him in heaven.

Jesus, thank You for dying for me on the cross.
You are the perfect Lamb of God. Amen.

BE A SERVANT LEADER

"But you will not be like that. Let the greatest among you be as the least. Let the leader be as the one who cares for others. Who is greater, the one who is eating at the table, or the one who is caring for him? Is it not the one who is eating at the table? But I am here with you as One Who cares for you."

LUKE 22:26–27

When you think of a king, what comes to mind? A golden crown with jewels? A purple robe? A throne? The Jews were expecting the Messiah to come as an earthly king. They never would have dreamed He would come as He did. They did not expect Him to be born in a stable, to be laid in a manger, or to grow up in a carpenter's shop. They didn't think he would ride into town on a donkey. They didn't expect His ministry to include meals with sinners.

When has anyone ever heard of a king who washes the feet of his subjects? But Jesus did that. He taught His followers to be servant leaders by His example. This is the type of leadership He modeled for them. He corrected them when they argued about who would be greatest in heaven. He told them that the greatest among them should care for others and should be as the least among them.

Lord, help me be a servant leader who cares for others. Amen.

JESUS FORGIVES SINS

Jesus said to him, "For sure, I tell you,
today you will be with Me in Paradise."

LUKE 23:43

What is the worst sin you can imagine? Hold that thought a moment. Now imagine that Jesus can forgive that sin. Jesus is ready and willing to pardon any sin anyone has committed if that person will repent, turn from sin, accept Him as Savior, and live a new life focused on the kingdom of God.

Jesus died an excruciating death as He hung between two criminals. The three men talked as they hung there on display. One man chose to trust in Jesus, and Jesus promised him he would be with Him in paradise that very day! Because of his faith, one criminal received eternal life before he died.

A life changed at a young age is even greater than one changed right before death! As a child, you likely have many years ahead of you. Come to Jesus while you are young so that you might receive the blessing of abundant life on this earth prior to the blessing of eternal life with Christ.

Lord, I believe You are able to forgive anyone's
sins. Thank You for forgiving mine. Amen.

KING OF THE JEWS

Then all the many people got up and took Jesus to Pilate.
They began to tell things against Him, saying, "We have
found this Man leading the people of our nation in a wrong
way. He has been telling them not to pay taxes to Caesar.
He has been saying He is Christ, a King." Pilate asked Jesus,
"Are You the King of the Jews?" He said, "What you said is true."

LUKE 23:1–3

Jesus was accused of leading the people away from their duties to the Roman government. This accusation was false. He was said to be telling the people not to pay their taxes. This accusation was false too. These were things that Jesus Christ simply did not do.

When Jesus was asked if He was the "King of the Jews," He answered truthfully. He said it was true. He is a King. He is the Jewish Messiah. He is the Savior of the world and the only Son of God, sent to make a way for people to come before a holy God.

But He was crucified upon a cross. The people, particularly the prideful, power-hungry leaders, wanted Him dead. He died the death used for criminals. He was hung to bleed and die between two thieves, on display for all to see. Nails pierced His flesh. How wrong this was, yet how right—because it was the only way to pay for our sins. The spotless Lamb of God took our sin upon Himself and willingly died on the cross.

Jesus, You are my King. Amen.

NO FAIR!

"After they received it, they talked against the owner. They said, 'The last workmen hired have only worked one hour. You have given to them the same as to us. We have worked hard through the heat of the day.'"

MATTHEW 20:11–12

The workers who had worked all day were mad because the landowner paid the workers who had only worked one hour a full day's wage—the same amount they earned. They weren't mad because they didn't get paid enough. They were mad because the newly hired workers were receiving, in their opinion, too much! It wasn't "fair."

First of all, this picture-story shows that no one can work their way to heaven. Salvation is a free gift from God.

It also reminds us that someone can come to know Christ in the last hours of her life on this earth and still receive eternal life. If this were not so, then we would have to believe that eternal life requires work, which it doesn't.

It's not fair. It is grace. Thank goodness it is not fair, or we would all get what we deserve: eternal separation from God!

Be thankful if you have come to know Christ early in life so that you may experience years of blessings from Him and service to Him. But never think for a moment that someone who is saved late in life doesn't deserve to see heaven's glory.

Lord, remind me every day that I am saved by
Your mercy—and not by anything I have done
or will do. Your salvation is a gift. Amen.

REJECTED IN NAZARETH

Jesus said to them, "One who speaks for God is respected everywhere but in his own country and among his own family and in his own house."

MARK 6:4

Does your family have close family friends? Do you also have many acquaintances (people who may not be as close but whom you speak to regularly) in your community? They know your parents, you, or your siblings, and soon they know the whole family.

This is how it was in Nazareth where Jesus grew up. People knew Him. They knew His mother, Mary. They knew Jesus worked alongside Joseph in the carpenter's shop. They had seen Him as a kid. It was hard for them to see Him as a Savior.

They did not believe.

Jesus had given them proof that He was the Son of God, so their choice was one they would be held accountable for (blamed for) in the end. He didn't waste any more time on the people of Nazareth. He went elsewhere to share the good news. How very sad for the Nazarenes that they did not recognize one of their own citizens as the one who could save them from their sins.

Lord, may I always know You. May I recognize Your hand in my life and sense when You are calling me to do something. I don't want to miss You, Jesus! Amen.

JESUS WONDERED AT THEIR UNBELIEF

So Jesus could do no powerful works there. But He did put His hands on a few sick people and healed them. He wondered because they had no faith. But He went around to the towns and taught as He went.

MARK 6:5–6

Have you ever been mistrusted or not believed? It feels awful, doesn't it? You stand there wondering how you can prove yourself trustworthy and honest. But in the end, it is up to the other individual. He must choose whether to believe you or not.

Jesus wondered because the people of Nazareth had no faith in Him. Other translations of this verse say that Christ was "amazed." It is the only place Mark says this about Jesus.

Jesus was shocked. He was taken aback. It was hard for Him to believe or accept that His own people, the Nazarenes, would reject Him. They could not see that He was the King, the Messiah, the long-awaited one.

Notice that Jesus did not stick around. When His message was rejected, He went to other towns. He shared the good news of salvation and the promise of eternal life with those who were ready to hear and accept.

Jesus, help me always to have faith and believe in You. Amen.

SHAKE THE DUST FROM YOUR FEET

"Whoever does not take you in or listen to you, when you leave there, shake the dust off your feet. By doing that, you will speak against them. For sure, I tell you, it will be easier for the cities of Sodom and Gomorrah on the day men stand before God and are judged than for that city."

MARK 6:11

There were customs and symbols in Jesus' day just as there are in modern times. The Jews would shake the dust off their clothing and sandals when they came back into Jewish territory after being in Gentile (non-Jew) territory. They did this because they believed the Gentiles' land was unclean.

Jesus told the disciples to use this same well-known action when they left people who didn't believe the good news they shared. Such people were unbelievers (pagans). When the disciples shook the dust off their feet as they left the area where such people lived, it meant that these people were to be rejected by their Master and the Father who had sent them. This act probably shook some of the pagans and caused them to reconsider their rejection of the gospel.

If you share the gospel with others but they reject the message of Christ and His offer of salvation, realize that this is not personal rejection. They are not shunning you but are shunning the Lord Himself.

Lord, may I boldly share the good news
regardless of whether others accept it. Amen.

NOTICE GODLY MARRIAGES

"Because of this, a man is to leave his father and mother and is to live with his wife. The two will become one. So they are no longer two, but one. Let no man divide what God has put together."

MARK 10:7–9

Have you ever made a pinky promise? Have you spit in your hand and mixed it with the spit of a buddy, becoming "brothers"? Have you made a promise to always be someone's friend?

Marriage is a covenant between the husband, the wife, and God. It is to be taken very seriously. It is a promise much more sacred than those made on the playground between friends. The man and woman are to leave their families and be together as a new family. They are to be fully committed to each other and not to turn to another man or woman for this same close relationship.

Remember as you watch the adults in your life to look for marriages that honor God. Do the husband and wife stay together? Do they read the Bible in their home? Do they attend church? Do they use their talents, abilities, and money to honor God? Such marriages are to be respected. They serve as a good model for you. Keep this in mind and take notes while you are young. Before you know it, you will be all grown up and deciding whom to marry! Be sure you look for a godly husband or wife.

Lord, thank You for marriages that honor You. Help me to notice men and women around me who are putting You first in their marriages. Amen.

LIKE A CHILD

"For sure, I tell you, whoever does not receive the holy nation of God as a little child does not go into it."

MARK 10:15

Have you ever heard of a great show or event coming to your town? You may ask someone how much the tickets cost only to be surprised when they answer, "It's free!"

When Jesus said that the kingdom of heaven was for those who received it with the faith of a child, the proud religious teachers and leaders could not believe it! They were shocked. They believed that their good works and the way they followed the law would get them into heaven. This was not so. Jesus taught a very different way.

Still today, many people believe that being good is the way to get to heaven. They may be far from Christ, but they try to do good works. They believe that the good things they do will save them a seat in heaven. This could not be further from the truth.

Tickets to heaven are not handed out based on what a person does. Eternal life with Jesus is a free gift granted to those who simply believe. Even a child can believe in Jesus.

Lord, thank You for the free gift of eternal life. My sins are forgiven because I have trusted in You! Amen.

JUMP UP AND FOLLOW JESUS

Jesus said to him, "What do you want Me to do for you?"
The blind man said to Him, "Lord, I want to see!" Jesus
said, "Go! Your faith has healed you." At once he
could see and he followed Jesus down the road.

MARK 10:51–52

May we all be like Bartimaeus, our brother in the Lord. He was a blind man, but even though he did not have physical sight, he had spiritual insight. Bartimaeus believed in Jesus, and he had faith that Jesus could heal him.

In Mark 10:47, we read that when this blind man heard that Jesus was coming, he boldly called out to Him. He called Him "Son of David."

Jesus healed Bartimaeus that day. He healed his eyes so that they were no longer blind. He also forgave his sins. And as Jesus left that place, we read that Bartimaeus followed Him.

The Bible tells us two important things about what Bartimaeus did when Jesus sent word for him to come to Him: Bartimaeus jumped up and threw off his coat. May we be quick to answer the call of Jesus. May we throw aside whatever may distract us. May we have the faith of this blind man who could see far better than the religious teachers of his day. He knew that Jesus was the Son of God!

Lord, may I follow You wholeheartedly, believing that You are the Son of God, just as Bartimaeus did. Amen.

ABOUT THE AUTHOR

Emily Biggers is a Tennessee native who resides in Texas. She works as an advanced academics specialist in a public school, teaching third-, fourth-, and fifth-grade students. She has one daughter, Lucy Carolina, who is the light of her life! She enjoys writing, decorating, taking beach vacations, playing with her black Lab named Bailey, and spending time with family and friends.

CHECK OUT THESE FANTASTICALLY FUN PRAYER MAPS!

 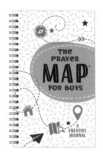

The Prayer Map for Girls
978-1-68322-559-1

The Prayer Map for Boys
978-1-68322-558-4

These prayer journals are a fun and creative way to more fully experience the power of prayer. Each page guides you to write out thoughts, ideas, and lists. . .which then creates a specific "map" for you to follow as you talk to God. Each map includes a spot to record the date, so you can look back on your prayers and see how God has worked in your life. *The Prayer Map* will not only encourage you to spend time talking with God about the things that matter most. . .it will also help you build a healthy spiritual habit of continual prayer for life!

Spiral Bound